# THE LETTER TO THE GALATIANS

# THE
# LETTER TO THE GALATIANS

## JOHN CARTER

THE CHRISTADELPHIAN
404 SHAFTMOOR LANE
HALL GREEN
BIRMINGHAM B28 8SZ

| First Edition | 1949 |
| Second Edition (reset) | 1977 |
| Third Edition (reset) | 2006 |

© 2006. The Christadelphian Magazine & Publishing Association Ltd

ISBN 0 85189 056 3

*Printed and bound in England by*
THE CROMWELL PRESS
Trowbridge
Wiltshire

# CONTENTS

# PREFACE

Of the letter to the Galatians it has been said: "There is nothing in ancient or modern language to be compared with this epistle. All the powers of Paul's soul shine forth in its few pages. Broad and luminous view, keen logic, biting irony, everything that is most forcible in argument, vehement in indignation, ardent and tender in affection, is found here, combined and poured forth in a single stream, forming a work of irresistible power".

Again and again the epistle has powerfully influenced men, and through men has affected the history of man. Luther was strongly moved by it, and by its teaching he assailed the errors and corruptions of the church in his day. He wrote and rewrote his commentary on the epistle, and the apostle's message moved men towards freedom from a bondage of ritual that was corrupt and corrupting.

The word of God is "living and powerful". It is a liberating power, but only as men read it and assimilate its message; then it leads to "the liberty of the children of God". For the New Testament writings are not simply sources for the history of the early days of Christianity, nor yet a source book for proof texts for doctrine. To limit the purpose of study to either of these objects is to miss much, and possibly to misunderstand. For proof texts must be read in the context, and history must take account of doctrine and of life, and above all, of the divine act in sending out the preachers with the message of life in the Son of God, crucified and risen and exalted.

Over many years the writer has studied the epistle to the Galatians. Three times courses of addresses have been given, in Bible Class, in Senior Class, in Study Group, and for each purpose the resumed study has brought deeper understanding. A further consideration for the purpose of writing this exposition intensifies the conviction that in God's word we have "unsearchable riches", which yet we must seek to know. As a possible help to others to understand in some measure this epistle of "our beloved brother Paul", "the Lord's ambassador to us Gentiles", this volume is published.

April, 1949                                                    JOHN CARTER

# GENERAL INTRODUCTION

IT is fortunate that the understanding of the general subject of an epistle of Paul does not depend upon a decision on the questions concerning when and to whom the letter was written. Nevertheless there are allusions to incidents and personal contacts which call for an enquiry into these questions if we are to understand all Paul's words. But sometimes his words admit of different explanations and there may be two views, both possible but not both correct. Yet some may think the balance of evidence is on one side, while others take the opposite view.

The discussions that have taken place by capable scholars, and the dogmatism with which rival views have been stated, might be thought sufficient reason for leaving the subject alone. But anyone who essays to write an exposition of the epistle is compelled to a decision.

## Galatia a Province

What is the difficulty, then, in determining who were the recipients of the letter to the Galatians? In the first place we observe that Galatia was not a town, like Corinth, Thessalonica, Philippi, Colosse or Rome. It was the name of a province, the boundaries of which were subject to frequent change. Hence the name can be used in a limited ethnographical sense and also in a political, administrative sense.

During the first quarter of the third century before Christ, a wave of Celtic invaders swept over Asia Minor, and for half a century they roamed and plundered at will. They were then confined by the king of Pergamum to a tract of land which was given the name of Galatia, in the northern part of the great central plateau of Asia Minor, and the three cities of Ancyra, Tavium and Pessinus were the centres of the three clans into which the Galatians were divided.

In 189 BC they were subdued by Roman arms, but during the Roman civil wars a native prince, Amyntas, acquired an extensive territory which Augustus allowed him to retain. On the death of Amyntas in 25 BC Galatia passed into the hands of the Romans. Some changes were made in the boundaries and the Roman province of Galatia was formed. The four cities of Antioch, Lystra, Derbe and Iconium were all included in this province, and all acquired importance in the defence system developed by Rome in the first half of the first century. These towns were separated by a great desert from the old Galatia which lay far to the north, but all four towns were built on the Roman road system which provided Paul easier travel than would have been possible at any time earlier, or much later. The people of these four towns, says Rackham, in his book on *Acts*,

"… had one point in common, they all belonged to the province of Galatia. In virtue of this their citizens — whether Phrygian or Lycaonian, Jewish or Greek, by birth — were all Galatians. Similarly, Trophimus who was of Ephesus, was an Asian, and Aristarchus of Thessalonica a Macedonian. The cities of Philippi, Thessalonica, and Berea were all in the province of Macedonia, and when Paul thinks of these churches together, he calls them the churches of Macedonia and their members Macedonians. Similarly, no doubt, when he wanted to speak of the churches of Antioch and Iconium, Lystra and Derbe, as one body, he would call them the churches of Galatia, and when he wrote to them in common he would address his readers as Galatians."

Over two centuries later the province was broken up, the effort of uniting heterogeneous peoples into a fictitious unity for political purposes being abandoned. The knowledge of the precise boundaries of the Roman province of Galatia was lost, and since the name was once again confined to the northern portion, readers of Paul's epistles easily fell into the view that the inhabitants of northern Galatia were those to whom Paul had written.

**The North Galatian View**

The view that the Galatia of Paul's letter was the old Celtic territory had an influence upon the interpretation of Acts and the assessment of Luke as a historian. Acts nowhere mentions a visit by Paul to the three towns of the northern Galatia, and only by straining language can a journey to that Galatia be included in Luke's history.

On Paul's first journey, after going through Cyprus the party crossed to the mainland of Asia Minor. Mark at once returned to Jerusalem, and Paul and Barnabas climbed up to the plateau, and came to Antioch of Pisidia. Expelled from there because of the success of their preaching, they went to Iconium. Here further dangers led them to go to the cities of

2

Lycaonia, Lystra and Derbe (Acts 13:14,51; 14:6). Antioch was given the description "of Pisidia" because it stood on the mountain slope looking down on Pisidia. It was a Phrygian city, at the time included in the Phrygian region of the Roman province of Galatia. Iconium was on the border of Lycaonia, but is correctly distinguished by Luke from the Lycaonian towns of Lystra and Derbe. All four towns, as we have said, were included in the Roman Galatia.

On the second journey, after the council at Jerusalem, Paul and Silas visited the cities where churches were founded; Luke then says: "And they went through the region of Phrygia and Galatia". The phrase means the region to which both "Phrygian" and "Galatian" apply, and this correctly describes the part of Phrygia that belonged politically to Galatia. In the words of Kirsopp Lake *(Earlier Epistles of Paul)*, "It is indeed hard to see what other district could be meant". Luke indicates that after visiting these cities the course of the party was directed to the port of Troas. They were hindered from turning right or left. Yet the North Galatian view is compelled to interpolate a long journey to northern Galatia and upset the natural force of Paul's words.

**The South Galatian View**

On the third journey Luke records that Paul "went through the region of Galatia in order, establishing all the disciples". From here he took the road to Ephesus (Acts 18:23; 19:1). A glance at a map showing the imperial roads and the political division of Paul's day makes it clear that the language again does not in any natural sense allow a visit to northern Galatia. To quote Kirsopp Lake again:

"Thus the meaning of the two passages in Acts in which a reference to 'Galatian' is found, points to the Churches of Derbe and Lystra as those covered by the expression 'the Galatic region' in 18:23, and Iconium and Antioch as those covered by 'the Phrygian and Galatic region' in 16:6. There is nothing in the Acts which need point to any other 'Galatian' Churches, and the theories which make Paul travel into the middle of the old Kingdom of Galatia are unsupported by the strict interpretation of Acts, and make Paul undertake long and dangerous journeys to sparsely populated regions, instead of keeping, as is far more probable, to the great roads and main centres of the Greek speaking population."

It should be added that in a later writing, in Vol. V of *The Beginnings of Christianity*, Lake does not speak so definitely as in this quotation.

On the North Galatia theory the earliest possible time for the writing of the letter to the Galatians would be between the second and third journeys. It is usually put late in the third journey. The first visit of Paul would then come after the Council of Jerusalem, where Paul accepted decrees and delivered them to the churches. It becomes very difficult, although many able scholars have felt compelled to essay the task, to reconcile this with Paul's declaration of his independence of the apostles and the account of his visits to Jerusalem in the epistle. No difficulty arises on the South Galatian view. On the latter theory the Galatian letter could have been written between the first and second journeys. The crisis in Galatia then belongs to the same circumstances that occasioned the Council at Jerusalem. If the letter was written at that time, Paul includes all his visits to Jerusalem prior to his visit to Galatia; and this is essential to his argument.

The interpretation of Galatians 1 and 2 in the following exposition is based upon this view. A detailed discussion of the many points involved in the rival theories can be examined in the older lives of Paul (Conybeare & Howson, Lewin, etc.) and in the many works of Sir Wm. Ramsay and others who have followed him. The persuasive advocacy of the South Galatian view by Ramsay, showing as it does the precise accuracy of Luke's writings in all his descriptions of towns and civic conditions, has not only won many adherents, but has led to a revision of the estimate in which Luke has been held as an historian. Instead of 'gaps' in his history, we find the accurate descriptions of an eye-witness of places and boundaries; we see Paul and his companions travelling the great arterial roads of the first century, planting lightstands at important centres from which the gospel radiated to remoter places. We see also the early rise of Jewish opposition; and the bitter conflict which arose from Gentiles being received as fellow disciples with the Jews. We see the prompt arraignment of the error and the vindication of the divine way of salvation by faith and not by works; by divine grace and not human actions; by the exclusion of human boasting and by the exaltation of the glory of God's mercy and grace.

# SECTION 1

## SALUTATION & INTRODUCTION (1:1–5)

THE opening words of this epistle have very great significance, for while they are a salutation, they also directly and abruptly introduce the issue to be discussed. Paul had taken the gospel to the Galatians, that is, as we believe, to those who formed the churches in Pisidian Antioch, Lystra, Derbe and Iconium. Barnabas was his companion, and it is almost certain that sickness had driven them into the highlands and so led to the preaching of Christ in those towns. The message of Paul and Barnabas had been received with joy and the messengers were regarded as sent by God.

On the return to Syrian Antioch "from whence they had been recommended to the grace of God for the work which they had fulfilled", they gathered the church together and rehearsed all that God had done with them. The "door of faith" had been opened to Gentiles, and it was manifest that the work begun there in preaching to Gentiles had God's approval. Slowly, and gradually, there had been extension of the work of proclaiming the good news: first in Jerusalem and Judea, then in Samaria. The prayers of Cornelius, a Gentile worshipper at the synagogue, had been heard by God, and Peter had used the 'key' given him by Jesus to open the door of knowledge of God's purpose to him. But it was Antioch that became the centre of the extended work, first in the preaching there, and then in the city becoming the home of a missionary enterprise in which the Spirit of God marked out Paul and Barnabas as appointed preachers. The whole development proved a great success, and a cause of joy and gladness.

But there were men who called themselves followers of Christ who viewed the extension of gospel work with disapproval, not because the gospel was preached to Gentiles, but because in this preaching "the cross of Christ" was put forward as the basis of salvation to the exclusion of the Law of Moses. The very basis of Jewish exclusiveness was thus done away, and with it the privileged position of Israel. This was

5

intolerable and steps were taken to checkmate Paul's labours.

## The Opposition of the Judaizers

It is probable that Jews of the Galatian towns Paul had visited brought to Jerusalem news of his activities. In Antioch of Pisidia they had stirred up the opposition of the rulers, who persecuted and expelled Paul; they had dogged his steps to other towns where the preachers were assaulted and stoned. On the visit to Jerusalem for one of the feasts these men would lay information about the new preaching. There were certain of "the sect of the Pharisees" who believed, and these men would hear from other Pharisees of the work of Paul, to their great annoyance and alarm. They therefore sent off men to Galatia to insist that Gentile converts to Christianity must be circumcised. Others were sent to the stronghold of the new work. In the words of Luke: "And certain men which came down from Judea (to Antioch) taught the brethren, and said, Except ye be circumcised after the manner of Moses, ye cannot be saved" (Acts 15:1).

In narrowing the issue to circumcision, the opponents of the gospel used a clever strategy. They could claim that the rite was not only based upon the Law but had an even older foundation. For Abraham received circumcision, and it was appointed to be the "sign" of the covenant. Paul saw that to concede the one point was to concede all, for if circumcision was essential, the whole system of outward forms and ceremonies was essential too, and salvation was by works or not at all. He said, "If ye be circumcised, Christ shall profit you nothing".

In Syrian Antioch the Judaizers were firmly resisted. Paul and Barnabas "had no small dissension and disputation with them" (Acts 15:2). But in Galatia the Judaizers were more successful and Paul's converts were quickly subverted. In order to overthrow his work the enemies of Paul had to undermine his personal authority. This they did with tragic results.

We do not know how news was brought to Paul, but if we have correctly outlined the position and placed events in a correct relationship, then news of the defection in Galatia came at the time of the contention in Antioch. Action had to be taken immediately, and the letter to the Galatians was written and sent off to counter the work of the destroyers of the gospel. In the letter Paul is revealed in all the intensity of his feeling, in his skill in argument, in his anxiety for his

6

converts, and in his own great loyalty and faithfulness to the gospel committed to him.

## Paul's Authority

His authority as Christ's ambassador had to be established, and the truth of his message that in Christ men were reconciled to God by faith vindicated. These two things are asserted in the opening words and are the key to the epistle: "Paul an apostle ... through Jesus Christ, who gave himself for our sins" (1:1,4).

"Paul an apostle (not of men, neither by man, but by Jesus Christ, and God the Father, who raised him from the dead;) and all the brethren which are with me, unto the churches of Galatia" (1:1,2). Paul, an apostle—the word apostle means one sent, an envoy, a commissioned messenger. The word is used particularly of "the twelve apostles of the Lamb" (Revelation 21:14; Matthew 10:2), for "of the disciples Jesus chose twelve, whom also he named apostles" (Luke 6:13). But the word has a wider usage. The brethren chosen by the Gentile churches to accompany Paul with the collection for the Jews at Jerusalem, are called "the apostles of the churches" (2 Corinthians 8:23), although the fact is disguised by the translation "messengers". These brethren were the appointed envoys of the churches. So Epaphroditus was the "messenger" or "apostle" of the Philippians, being sent to visit Paul in prison (Philippians 2:25). Paul and Barnabas are called "apostles" in Acts 14:4,14, perhaps particularly because they were "sent" by the Holy Spirit, "separated" for the work among the Gentiles. This commission directly decreed of God gave Paul and Barnabas an unquestioned position of authority and responsibility among the Gentile churches. But Paul's apostleship had an even stronger foundation than the commission given him and Barnabas at Antioch. Paul was a chosen vessel; and as he came to recognise, he "was separated from his mother's womb", though much later "called by God's grace" to be the bearer of that grace to others hitherto regarded as outside its operation. While God's own Son was growing up in a village in Galilee increasingly recognising the work for which God had sent him, another boy was being prepared to be linked with that work, but all unknowing. In fact the preparation was completed, paradoxical though it may be, in his bitter efforts to destroy the faith which it was his work to establish. Thus, while pursuing to "strange cities" the followers of the Nazarene, he was apprehended by their Lord who was thus found, as they claimed, to be indeed raised from the

7

dead—a divinely vindicated Lord and not the impostor Paul had thought him to be.

## Paul's Witness to the Resurrection

It seems a feasible interpretation of 2 Corinthians 5:16 that Paul had known Jesus during his ministry. One cannot think of a man like Paul, a leading pupil of Gamaliel, and one who had an important place in the councils of the nation when only about thirty, not knowing of the excitement and enthusiasm which the new prophet had caused. He must have visited Jerusalem for one of the feasts during the three years Jesus was preaching. There would thus be a personal recognition that the glorious person whose brightness blinded him was indeed Jesus of Nazareth. That meeting with Jesus was the ultimate authority of Paul's apostleship, for then he was appointed as a chosen vessel to bear Christ's name to the Gentiles. When gainsayers in Corinth cast doubts upon his standing, he advanced as proof of his apostleship the meeting with Jesus. "Have I not seen the Lord Jesus? Are not ye our work in the Lord?" (1 Corinthians 9:1,2). In this respect then, Paul was not a whit behind the chiefest apostle, though his enemies did rudely call him an "abortion" (1 Corinthians 15:8).

From the first it was recognised as a qualification of apostleship in the primary sense, that a man must be a witness to the resurrection (Luke 24:48 with Acts 1:8). He must have direct personal knowledge of the most fundamental fact of their preaching. The outstanding marks of an apostle are his personal knowledge of the risen Christ; his reception, by the Spirit, of truth to be authoritatively proclaimed to others; the possession of miraculous powers with the power to impart to others; and the authority to enforce discipline. In all respects Paul was equal to those who together are called "The Twelve" (1 Corinthians 15:5).

The issue had been raised among the Galatians that Paul had not the qualifications of an apostle as Peter and John had; his apostleship, such as it was, was secondary and derived. This derogation is countered at once in the parenthesis of verse 1. He was not an apostle appointed of men, not even of The Twelve, nor by a man, as Barnabas or James; neither the source nor the channel was human; and the change from "men" to "a man", from the corporate body to an individual, leads on to the One from whom he had received his commission: "Not by a man—but by Jesus Christ and God the Father, who raised him from the dead". It is true Jesus was a man, but he was more; he was the Son of God, indicated here by Paul calling God "the Father"; and Jesus Christ, who appointed Paul, had the divine endorsement, for he was risen from the dead. The words are an emphatic assertion that he was an apostle by divine appointment. The proof of it he advances later in the epistle when he rebuts the false insinuations that had been made about him.

## An Abrupt Introduction

It was customary for Paul to join the names of others with his own in the address of his letters. Here he stands named alone, for the emphatic personal assertion of his apostleship was necessary. Yet he joins others unnamed with himself in the address: "All the brethren who are with me." In itself the phrase is ambiguous, which accounts for the many suggestions that have been made concerning who are intended by it. Explanations are influenced by the view which may be held concerning the place where the epistle was written and who would be with Paul at the time. If the suggestion already made that the letter was written from Antioch at the time of the agitation caused by the Jerusalem Judaizers is correct, then the natural meaning is that the phrase refers to the general body of the church in Antioch. "All the brethren with" Paul, then contrasts with the teachers who were Paul's opponents and any who may sympathise with them. Ramsay quotes with approval the words of Dr. Zöckler, who explains Paul's words:

"The whole body of fellow Christians who were with him at the time (not merely his more prominent helpers) are mentioned by Paul as those who join with him in greeting the Galatians. He does this in order to give the more emphasis to what he has to say to them. He writes indeed with his own hand (6:13) but in the name of a whole great Christian community. The warnings and exhortations which are to be addressed to the Galatians go forth from a body whose authority cannot be lightly regarded."

Very abruptly Paul concludes the opening sentence: "to the church of Galatia". The absence of any such phrases as "in God the Father and the Lord Jesus Christ" (1 Thessalonians 1:1) or "sanctified in Christ Jesus, called to be saints" (1 Corinthians 1:2), is to be noted. There is no expression of praise, no thanksgiving, no word of commendation or love. When we remember how warmly the apostle expresses his appreciation of the hope, faith and love of his converts, the severity of the Galatian letter shows how deeply the apostle felt their defection, and how serious was the effect of their change of belief. "To be circumcised" or "not to be circum-

9

cised" may seem battle-cries of a far off conflict, yet they touch deep principles which affect men's salvation.

## Grace and Peace

Paul's feelings for the Galatians, nonetheless, are of the strongest and the highest. Always mindful of his apostleship —that by him the gospel of God might be preached in the world—he therefore does not fail to write the benediction which is part of the salutation in his letters: "Grace unto you and peace from God the Father, and from our Lord Jesus Christ." The word "grace" used by Paul is related to the word for 'greeting' in common speech in Paul's day. But the adaptation of it made by Paul infuses a fuller meaning into the word than the casually and often flippantly and thoughtlessly expressed greeting, by which Greek hailed Greek in any of the streets of the world of Paul's day. "Grace", in Paul's use, expresses the mercy and favour of God, particularly God's favour to Gentiles. Paul always retained the wonder that he felt when he understood that God's purpose and grace included both Gentile and Jew; and especially when he knew that God had made him the channel by which His mercy should be made known to the Gentiles. Grace comprehends all the blessing made available in God's kindness in providing salvation for sinful men and women. Fickle and unstable the Galatians had shown themselves for the moment; their folly is to be exposed, but they therefore needed "grace" all the more.

To grace is added "peace". The one is derived from Greek, the other from Hebrew custom. "Peace" (*shalom*) was the greeting used by the Jew—perhaps an echo of the high-priestly blessing of Numbers 6:23–26: "The LORD bless thee … and give thee peace". It was used by the Jew in a very conventional way day by day, generally without appreciation of the beauty and restfulness of the blessing. When Jesus spoke of his peace that he would leave with his disciples, he declared it was not as the world gave peace. The way men said "Peace" was empty of real desire, being merely opening or closing words by which man accosted man. Jesus had peace to give, dearly bought by him if we think of the fullest significance of the word. "Being justified by faith, we have peace with God" (Romans 5:1); and peace with God brings inward peace.

Paul lifts these words of common greeting up to their highest level by adding to them "from God the Father and our Lord Jesus Christ". His words are a prayer that God's grace, which had been revealed in His Son, should be theirs, and that with it they might therefore know peace.

## Christ a Sacrifice for Sin

This exalted significance is at once apparent from the sequence, for Paul declares that the Lord Jesus Christ "gave himself for our sins, that he might deliver us from this present evil world, according to the will of God and our Father". To add these words to the greeting and then restrict the meaning of the greeting to that which was generally spoken without care and thought, would take all value out of the added words.

These words, however, do more than infuse the benediction with a full meaning. They bear directly upon the troubles in the Galatian churches. The grace of God was something freely bestowed because it was not in man's power to earn it. But while free, it did not spring from a generous act of good feeling such as may prompt men to exercise benevolence without regard to principle or consequence. The grace of God was provided in a way consonant with His character, with moral principles maintained and exhibited at every stage of God's work, and with the express object of producing certain required consequences in and for men.

The Lord Jesus "gave himself for our sins". Our sins are the great difficulty in our relationship to God. We are not able to say, 'Let them be forgotten', as easy-going emotional people may think it should be possible. Neither can God say, 'Let us think no more about them'—unless certain conditions are satisfied. The popular temper today may wish God to be like 'a benevolent uncle' only concerned about bestowing those things that men want. This is a mark of the shallow thinking of much that passes for religious teaching today. Even where there is some mental effort to explain the work of Jesus in offering himself, a growing number of writers reduce his death to a kind of heroic martyrdom which is set forth to provoke men to abjure sin and seek after righteousness.

It is futile, however to attempt to understand how the work of Jesus is related to our sins and our salvation unless we take the Scripture's explanation, for only in that way can we know God's mind. Human speculation will get us nowhere; divine revelation will enable us to understand the character of God revealed in the sacrifice of His Son.

## The Cross Destroys Justification by Works

Jesus "*gave* himself for our sins". So saying, Paul brings to view the historical facts connected with Christ's death as he had preached them to the Galatians. Though not a witness of the crucifixion, Paul had vividly realised that on the cross Jesus had wrought that which was of infinite benefit to Paul himself. Apprehending its meaning, he had seen the futility of his own striving for a meritorious righteousness by law; the very fact of God's provision of a Son so to die was the final disproof of the Jewish attitude of trying to gain God's favour by keeping the law. Paul, therefore, became dead to law to live unto God; he was crucified with Christ that he might live "by the faith of the Son of God, who loved me and gave himself for me" (Galatians 2:20). The phrase "gave himself" might in another context be ambiguous: a person can spend his strength to help another and so give himself: but in Paul's use, as is evident by the sense in the passage quoted, the words can mean nothing less than that Jesus voluntarily laid down his life in crucifixion.

"He *gave* himself": Paul was very conscious of the intensely personal quality of the Lord's "offering for sin". While he relates the Lord's offering to the will of God, and to the righteousness of God, and on occasion explains it in terms of unplumbed depths, he yet always is aware that the bearing of the cross was a real laying down of a man's life. The reasons for it are truly connected with the holiness of God, and because of "our sins", "our offences", "our transgressions" and "our iniquities". But in giving the reasons for God's arrangements for man's redemption; Paul never loses sight of what this involved for Jesus himself, and of the personal surrender Jesus made in the great task laid upon him. He "loved me"; "The love of Christ constraineth me"; "Christ died for the ungodly"; "Who is he that condemneth? It is Christ that died"; "Who shall separate us from the love of Christ?" This language describes personal feeling and personal action, realised more when we remember that the love of Christ entailed suffering; he "endured the cross, despising the shame"; "he endured contradiction of sinners against himself"; "he himself hath suffered"; "he learned obedience by the things he suffered". These are but illustrations of the Apostle's language which show his strong grasp of the personal aspect of the work of Jesus: and the reference to them will prevent us from overlooking the wealth of meaning and of feeling in the simple words: "He—gave—himself."

**Forgiveness and Reconciliation**

"Our Lord Jesus Christ ... gave himself for our sins." The forgiveness of sins through Christ was at the forefront of the message of the apostles. "I delivered unto you first of all", says Paul to the Corinthians, "that which I also received, how

12

that Christ died for our sins according to the scriptures" (1 Corinthians 15:3). We see the important sense that attaches to Paul's statement that his message was one he had received personally and directly when he says: "All things are of God, who hath reconciled us to himself by Jesus Christ and hath given to us the ministry of reconciliation; to wit, that God was in Christ, reconciling the world unto himself, not imputing their trespasses unto them; and hath committed unto us the word of reconciliation. Now then we are ambassadors for Christ, as though God did beseech you by us: we pray you in Christ's stead, be ye reconciled to God" (2 Corinthians 5:18–20).

God had given to Paul this ministry among the Gentiles, and upon the basis of God's work in Christ men were urged to be reconciled to God. Reconciliation was assured because trespasses were not imputed; in Christ sins were forgiven. In describing this forgiveness and the means whereby it had become possible, Paul and the other apostles use a wide range of terms and employ a variety of figures of speech. This variety of expression was made possible by the preparatory work of the law of God as a code of instruction to Israel. The ritual law used a wide vocabulary in describing the various offerings and enjoined quite a range of words in the confessions that were required. Offerings were for sin and trespass; on the Day of Atonement the high priest confessed over the head of the live goat which was sent away into the wilderness, the iniquities, transgressions and sins of the people. The Jews were thus familiar with terms by which they could describe actions which were contrary to God's law. The ritual, being typical and part of the preparation for Christ's coming, inevitably gave the form to the vocabulary by which the offering of Christ was described. In recognising this we must guard against the thought that since the language was borrowed from the types, it does not describe real facts when used of Jesus.

### The Term "Blood"
The work of Jesus is explained in the terms of the law because the law was given to instruct the people of God concerning the principles which govern man's relationship to God—principles which must be recognised as the condition of man's return to God's favour. This is illustrated in the use of the term "blood". The blood of animals figured in several ways in the law's appointments; in the consecration of the high priest and on the Day of Atonement, are two of the most important. But the law instructed the Israelites that the

blood was not to be eaten because "the life of the flesh is in the blood: and I have given it to you upon the altar to make an atonement for your souls: for it is the blood that maketh atonement for the soul" (Leviticus 17:11). The blood was the life stream, and in ritual use became a symbol of the life offered. When then Jesus speaks of "my blood" and of "the blood of the new covenant shed for the remission of sins", and when Paul speaks of "the blood of Christ", they are using the terminology of the law with its ritual significance to describe the laying down of Christ's life. It is literally true that Christ's blood was poured out in that his hands and feet and side were pierced: but the essential fact is that life was given. This is evident when we consider that his blood was not literally taken into the Holiest as the blood of animals was sprinkled on the mercy seat by the High Priest on the Day of Atonement. His blood, as red fluid, stained his hands and dropped on the soil where he was crucified. It had no magical value, such as Roman Catholics have attached to it. Something very real was, nevertheless, done through Christ's death, something of which the high priest's entry into the holiest was a foreshadowing. That reality is, however, expressed by Paul in words taken from the type: "By his own blood he entered in once into the holy place, having obtained eternal redemption"; and in other words which expound the type when he says: "For Christ is not entered into the holy places made with hands, which are the figures of the true; but into heaven itself, now to appear in the presence of God for us" (Hebrews 9:24).

We may re-state the matter thus. In the shadow arrangements the high priest entered the holiest with shed blood: in the reality thus foreshadowed, Jesus entered into the presence of the Father through his own voluntary death. Even so, we have only stated the fact and left undefined the moral principle upon which the fact was established.

**Parallel Statements**

Returning to the consideration of Paul's language that it was "for our sins" that Jesus gave himself, we may note the following statements which are valuable for comparison. "He was delivered for our offences" (Romans 4:25); "He offered one sacrifice for sins" (Hebrews 10:12); "Christ also hath once suffered for sins" (1 Peter 3:18); "Christ was once offered to bear the sins of many" (Hebrews 9:28); "Who his own self bare our sins in his own body on the tree" (1 Peter 2:24); "It behoved Christ to suffer, and to rise from the dead the third day: and that repentance and remission of sins should be preached in his name among all nations, beginning at Jerusalem" (Luke 24:46,47); "Through his name whosoever believeth in him shall receive remission of sins" (Acts 10:43); "Through this man is preached unto you the forgiveness of sins" (Acts 13:38); "In whom we have redemption through his blood, the forgiveness of sins, according to the riches of his grace" (Ephesians 1:6,7, see also Colossians 1:13,14). It is a fitting ascription that the redeemed utter to the praise of the Lamb: "Unto him that loved us, and washed us from our sins in his own blood, and hath made us kings and priests unto God and his Father; to him be glory and dominion for ever and ever" (Revelation 1:5,6).

The forgiveness of sins is essential, or none would be saved: but more than that is necessary, for forgiveness expresses only one side of the redemptive work of Jesus. Paul therefore adds that "He gave himself ... that he might deliver us from this present evil world according to the will of God". The "world" is the age in which we live, transitory and evil—the domain of sin. Another age is spoken of by Jesus— "that age and the resurrection of the dead"—to which men may attain if counted worthy. Men who shape their way of life by the forms and practices of their contemporaries who are not governed by God's law but their own desires, will not be worthy. The first step in the emancipation from the present order is to recognise it as evil: that the world lieth in the wicked one. This recognition comes as part of an awareness of the sinfulness of human nature, as seen in one's own self, which knowledge of God's truth brings home to a man. He sees himself as part of a world under the dominion of sin: he feels himself in its grip; but he is powerless to deliver himself. Then he finds that the one in whom is forgiveness is also the emancipator, able now to "deliver" the captive from the power that holds in thrall. He is not taken out of the world as a physical environment, but he is kept from the evil (John 17:15), and his daily prayer becomes "Deliver us from evil". That Paul is thinking of the clause in the Lord's prayer seems practically certain when he defines Christ's work further to forgiveness as deliverance from "this present evil world".

**The Will of God**

One more phrase in the introductory verses calls for attention. Paul declares that Jesus gave himself for our sins that he might deliver us from the present evil world "according to the will of God and our Father". The will of God is the primary cause of the work of redemption: because of His will it

15

was necessary for Jesus to give himself that our sins might be forgiven and deliverance from evil effected.

The fact that all that has been done for man's salvation is of God is declared in many places in the apostolic writings. "Of God, Jesus is made unto us wisdom, and righteousness, and sanctification, and redemption" (1 Corinthians 1:30).

In Psalm 40 David indicated that animal offerings of all kinds were inadequate to effect redemption. Speaking by "the spirit of Christ which was in him" (1 Peter 1:11), and therefore using words that can only properly come from the lips of Christ himself, he declared that because God "did not desire" the offerings of animals, the Christ came to do God's will. "Then said I, Lo, I come, in the volume of the book it is written of me, I delight to do thy will, O my God: yea, thy law is within my heart." How impossible for David to say concerning himself that his obedience to God was written in the volume of God's book! While he was a man after God's own heart, as God Himself testified, yet there were actions in his life which marred the record. In the pregnant sense of the Psalm, David's coming could not be said to have been "to do God's will". Also, it could not be said of him that he had been the subject of prophecy throughout the revelation of God's purpose. Only of the Messiah can such language be used. But this application to the Messiah, which springs from the necessities of the language itself, is expressly confirmed by Paul's application of the verses in Hebrews 10:5–9, to which Paul adds, "By the which will (of God) we are sanctified through the offering of the body of Jesus Christ once for all" (verse 10).

But the will of God extends beyond the personal work of Jesus—it embraces all the effects of that work upon men who believe. Paul speaks of the Ephesians being "predestinated unto the adoption of children by Jesus Christ to himself, according to the good pleasure of his will" (Ephesians 1:5), "the mystery of his will having been made known" (verse 9), and therefore God "worketh all things after the counsel of his own will that we should be to the praise of his glory, who first trusted in Christ" (verses 11,12). While Paul thus never loses sight of God's action in Christ and of the sovereign will that called for the offering of Jesus, there was a particular reason for the assertion in these opening verses of the letter to the Galatians, that Jesus gave himself according to the will of God. The thought is essential to the vindication of Paul's gospel in opposition to the teaching of the Judaizers.

## God our Father

Before we gather up the ideas of these opening verses which challenge the falsehoods to be exposed throughout the letter, we must notice that Paul described God as "our Father". The RV has "God our Father" in the margin of verse 3; and in verse 4 attaches the pronoun to both God and Father—"our God and Father". Later in the epistle Paul shows that the belief of the gospel introduces the believer to the status of sons; the man who is simply a law-keeper is a slave. As God, the Almighty gives laws; but His Fatherhood is not revealed by law.

There have been two penal laws in past dispensations. The first was in Eden where the declared consequence of disobedience was death. No other member of the race has stood in exactly the same position as Adam in Eden, for Adam's disobedience not only affected himself but all his posterity. Death came to Adam at the end of 930 years; but after transgression, in all those years he laboured with sweat of face to produce his food, and knew sorrow and sadness and the weakness of mortality. Paul affirms that death "passed upon all men" by Adam's sin (Romans 5:12). The language is emphatic, as is also the statement: "by man came death"; and this death is evidently the death which ends the present life, for Paul adds "by man came also the resurrection of the dead". Christ raised from death is the firstfruits raised from the death that reigns through Adam's sin.

The other penal code was the Mosaic, which contained certain clauses, transgression of which had to be punished with death. Since the Mosaic code was a rule of life given as an essential part of the covenant which the Israelites agreed to obey, failure to keep any part brought the curse of the law upon the offender. The Galatians were being seduced into accepting an imposition of this code as a condition of salvation; they were accepting what would curse and not bless; and doing this they were falling from the status of "sons" to "slaves".

In these opening verses, then, Paul has asserted as against his traducers that his apostleship was not of men but by the risen Jesus and God the Father. His authority has the highest sanctions. The gospel that he taught, and which the Galatians had received from him, was good news of the forgiveness of sins through Christ's sacrifice and of escape from an evil world. The gospel was an exhibition of God's way of salvation, by God's grace and not by human merit. If the offering of Jesus was according to God's will then that

17

offering was essential for salvation. The imposition by the Judaizers of other conditions implied that the arrangements God made in the gift of His Son and in that Son giving himself, were not sufficient for their redemption. The very fact that God spared not His own Son that men might have life is of itself an end once for all of the notion that Adam's descendants could get eternal life by keeping the Law of Moses or any other legal code. The gospel introduced men into a relationship to God through His Son whereby they too were recognised as sons of God, and could call on God as Father.

Paul's opponents charged him with being but an emissary of the Twelve, and in addition with having perverted the gospel given to him. The Twelve, they said, were appointed by Jesus—but Paul was a late comer: and his authority was not original but derived. His opponents declared that believers must be circumcised to become members of "the common-wealth of Israel and of the household of God". Paul saw that to accept circumcision as an essential condition of salvation involved keeping the whole law also. The law brought neither grace nor peace, forgiveness nor sonship. It brought bondage and not deliverance.

The ideas thus indicated in the opening verses are elaborated in the letter. The facts of history are with Paul. He had seen Christ; he knew Jesus was raised from the dead; he knew himself the grace and peace he invoked for his readers; he knew that the facts of the history of Jesus were an unfolding of God's will for the forgiveness of men's sins; and therefore "To God be glory for ever and ever" (verse 5).

# SECTION 2

## PAUL'S DEFENCE OF HIS APOSTLESHIP
### THE INTOLERANCE OF THE GOSPEL (1:6–9)

THE usual form of letter writing in the first century began with salutation, followed by thanksgiving. From the great number of illustrations available from the papyri discoveries in Egypt, three or four examples are given in the exposition of the *Letter to the Ephesians* (page 35).* Paul generally followed the customary arrangement, often lifting contemporary expressions from a conventional and thoughtless use to be the means of expressing the highest and noblest thought. Even in his first letter to the Corinthians—which deals with so many troubles and difficulties, all giving Paul great cause for anxiety—the apostle follows the greeting with the words: "I thank my God always on your behalf, for the grace of God which is given you by Jesus Christ" (1 Corinthians 1:4). The absence of such a thanksgiving in the Letter to the Galatians shows not only how deeply the apostle felt the change in the Galatian believers, but also how serious was their defection from the gospel. The doctrine of the Judaizers, while claiming to complete the gospel, was really opposed to it. If their claim was true the gospel was an ineffectual means of salvation. Paul saw this clearly, and his stern words are a reflection of the seriousness of the position in Galatia.

Instead, then, of a sentence beginning "I thank God", we find: "I marvel that ye are so quickly removing from him that called you in the grace of Christ unto a different gospel." Defection had been quick, not only from the shortness of the interval from the time the gospel was preached to them, but also in the rapidity with which they had yielded to the demands of the new teachers. Those who think the Galatians addressed in the letter were dwellers in North Galatia, regard the latter as the meaning because of the length of time that elapsed between Paul's preaching and the writing of the letter. But if the churches addressed were in South Galatia, the former meaning is the natural one. The Galatians had not long held the course, and this in view of the enthusiasm

---

* These examples are on page 41 of the Second Edition of this work.

with which they had received the gospel filled the apostle with indignant surprise.

## The Repeal of the Law

"Him that called you" is God, to whose will Paul has in the preceding verse ascribed the whole purpose of grace. The Judaizers doubtless made much of the fact that the law was of God and that it should be observed by all. But God who gave the law to Israel had called Gentiles "into the grace of Christ". The law was national; and if in former times a Gentile, like Ruth or Rahab, laid hold of the hope of Israel, they became citizens of Israel. In the absence of the repeal of the law, Jews who believed in Jesus continued to keep also the law. During the period of history practically covered by the Acts of the Apostles, this was the case; but the letter to the Hebrews, after establishing that God had spoken in a Son in whom all the foreshadowings of the law found their fulfilment, called upon even Hebrew believers to join Christ "without the camp" of Israel. This purpose in large measure explains the anonymity of the Hebrews letter: by the absence of the writer's name the letter has the sanction of divine authority without any intermediary. This change of the relationship of the Jewish believer to the Law was gradual, as was appropriate to the circumstances. The preaching of the gospel accompanied by a demand to abandon the law would have closed all Jewish ears to God's invitation. The divine repeal in the letter to the Hebrews preceded by only a short time the insurrection which resulted in the destruction of the city and temple by the Romans, by which the keeping of the law became impossible in many respects.

While, then, as a practical measure, Jews adhered to Jewish ways for a time, the demand that Gentiles should adopt their forms of worship and ceremonial was an imposition of a typical thing upon the reality typified. This virtually made the gospel to be ineffectual without the law, and the Jewish preachers were therefore preaching another gospel.

The word *another* in verses 6 and 7, represents two words in the Greek, and the RV has attempted to preserve the distinction by *different* in verse 6. Much has been written about the precise significance of the two words; that they are synonyms when used separately is admitted by all, but some writers insist that a distinction is intended when the words are used in close connection. The precise distinction—which word defines only numerical difference (another of the same class), and which essential difference (one of another class)—

is a disputed point; its detailed consideration would not be of general profit.

## A "different" Gospel

The sense may be as follows: the Judaizers were preaching a different gospel; to Paul it was essentially different—so much so that he denies its right to the term gospel: it is another gospel, for there cannot be two gospels; his gospel and the gospel of his opponents were mutually exclusive. It could, in fact, be only called another gospel in the sense that the Judaizers were perverting their minds and overthrowing the true gospel. What a work to describe as a gospel!

This interpretation may then also be understood as meeting assertions made by the Judaizers, who said Paul's gospel was really a modification of the original gospel which he had received of the twelve. Paul retorts that he preaches the true gospel—this other, to which the Galatians were now giving heed, is no gospel at all; and before dealing with the vital question of the source of his gospel, he declares that so authoritative was the gospel he preached that anyone proclaiming any other gospel was accursed. It is strong language, with the emphasis of repetition: "As we have said before, so say I now again, If any man preach any other gospel unto you than that ye have received, let him be accursed". Some said that Paul had trimmed in certain actions, and in part of his teaching; if so, he was included in the anathema; but the consistency of his course he will defend. But since Judaizers asserted a difference in their teaching and Paul's, they were anathema.

It would be easy to explain the vehemence of these words as arising simply from the strength of Paul's feelings; but when we consider what the effects would have been if Paul had not won this battle of Galatia, we can attach to them all the weight that belongs to their face value—all of which Paul intended.

The gospel is for men's salvation, and is a revelation of God's will. A perversion of the gospel misrepresents God's will and takes away knowledge of salvation. A perverter of the gospel is a destroyer of the true hope—he is one who throws away the key of knowledge and leaves closed the door by which men can enter into the Kingdom of God.

## The Truth of Paul's Gospel

Paul was certain of the truth of his gospel. His confidence had a starting point in his experience in meeting the Christ; but the conviction then produced was fortified by two things.

There was first the evidence provided by the Old Testament writings that the Christ must suffer and rise again. The evidence was abundant and it was clear, both in its broad definitions of the work of the Servant of God, whose life was to be an offering for sin, and also in the amount of detail revealed concerning the outward circumstances that would be connected with the death of the Messiah. There was also the evidence of the continual witness of the Holy Spirit, both in the power which it conferred upon Paul and also in the manifestation of spirit gifts among those who believed. The assurance of Paul, epitomised in his words, "I know whom I have believed, and am persuaded that he is able to keep that which I have committed unto him against that day" (2 Timothy 1:12), is justified. It would be a mistake, however, to attribute to that confidence in the truth of his gospel what might be called the intolerance expressed in the words, "Though we, or an angel from heaven, preach any other gospel unto you than that which we have preached unto you, let him be accursed".

The sentiments of this statement are altogether out of keeping with the popular spirit today in matters of religion. A man may be permitted a complete absorption in a political theory, but boldness and assertion in setting forth Christian doctrine is frowned upon. The evolutionist can indulge in dogmatic utterances and find approval; a similar dogmatism about revealed doctrine is regarded as a mark of narrow-mindedness.

Yet if the gospel is true, an intolerance is inevitable. If God has spoken, His word must not be contradicted. If God should raise up among men a prophet and "put His words into his mouth" to "speak all that God has commanded him", it is basically right that God should impose the penalty of broken law upon the disobedient. "It shall come to pass, that whosoever will not hearken unto my words which he shall speak in my name, I will require it of him" (Deuteronomy 18:19).

God said to Israel. "Thou shalt have no other gods before me" (Exodus 20:3). The Holy One of Israel, the living God, cannot share the reverence and worship of men with false gods which men have devised for themselves—with idols of wood and stone. What is true of God Himself is true also of His redemptive work for men. If God should reveal glad tidings of good for men, whatever perverts that gospel makes God a liar, and substitutes human folly for divine wisdom. When in the outworking of that purpose God manifests Himself in a man who is both son of man and son of God, and then in accordance with God's revealed will that Son suffers and dies that God in His mercy may forgive the sins of men, any substitution of another suggested way flouts the Creator's act of love. Denial of the gospel, whether outright or implicit, in the substitution of a doctrine which undermines it, can only call for divine judgement and the resistance of men who are faithful to God's word.

The man who destroys the gospel is the enemy of God and of his own fellows. He antagonises God's purposes and deprives men of the way of salvation. As God is one, so the gospel is one, as Paul claims in Romans 3:30. Any other 'gospel' is false and its promoters must be anathema.

## God's Way is Exclusive

The emphatic exclusiveness of God's way revealed in the Bible is unpalatable to the modern mind, but the general attitude of men to God's Word must be reprehensible to God. It is revealed that God is a jealous God. If He did not assert His supremacy it would be tantamount to an abdication, which would be as impossible as it is for God to deny Himself. The exclusiveness also comes out in countless utterances. "My glory will I not give to another." "I will be sanctified in them that approach unto me." "There is none other name given under heaven whereby we must be saved." "Neither is there salvation in any other." "He that hath the Son hath life: he that hath not the Son of God hath not life." "No man knoweth the Son but the Father: neither knoweth any man the Father, save the Son, and he to whomsoever the Son will reveal him" (Matthew 11:27). "If we say we have not sinned we make him a liar, and his word is not in us." These are but samples; almost every page of the Bible supplies others.

A man denies an obvious mathematical statement, and he displays a dullness of intellect. But if a man denies the essential truths of salvation when they are made known in a revelation authenticated as true by many evidences, his fault passes from the intellectual to the moral plane. As it is a moral fault to deny God's way, it becomes a moral necessity to uphold it. Its defence and maintenance is nothing less than taking the side of God, and a refusal to do so is joining the enemies of God.

The declarations of anathema by Paul, then, is not a product of fanatical vehemence, but belongs of necessity to the fact that his gospel is God's good news. Paul saw clearly that his opponents, in subverting his gospel, were taking away God's saving knowledge from his converts, and were putting in the place what was no gospel at all. With this, to steal a man's purse was not comparable.

An argument from another point of view is derivable from Paul's statement. That Paul should pronounce anathema on a perverter of his gospel shows how fundamental, how essential, how true, is his message. The denial of the casual and the trivial impose no such terrible consequences. The pronouncement of anathema, then, is an appropriate indication, in the face of the perversion of it by his Judaizing opponents, that his gospel was true.

## PAUL'S GOSPEL REVEALED BY CHRIST (1:10–12)

PAUL'S hurried sentences, which yet never cease to be logical and cogent, sometimes defy an ordered analysis. We have included verse 10 with this section, but it could equally well have been included in the last section. Some divide the text at verse 9; the RV ends the paragraph at verse 10; but wherever we make the division Paul's thought runs on.

At this point in his letter Paul begins his defence of himself, of his integrity, of the genuineness of his message—this portion of the letter reaching to the end of chapter 2.

It has been well remarked that in the letters of Paul we have echoes of his opponents' words. Sometimes he takes up the very phrases of their argument, and unless we discern these references our understanding of his reply will suffer. Anyone interested to test the matter might read the letters to the Corinthians as translated by Conybeare and Howson, and observing the quotation marks note how much is gained in force and clarity. It might be possible to show an excess of zeal in thus attributing phrases to Paul's opponents, but that does not require us to ignore the obvious illustrations of the fact. Ramsay quotes Prof. W. Locke to the effect that "in order to comprehend many passages in Paul's letters, we must understand that certain phrases represent the substance, if not the actual words, of the taunts levelled in speech against him by his Jewish Christian opponents". Galatians 1:10 provides a good illustration of this.

The enemies of Paul's gospel accused the apostle of accommodating his gospel to his hearers that he might win converts. To find their words perverted and misused is the experience of all who preach the gospel and who in so doing expose heresy. Paul suffered much in this way. He himself said that he became all things to all men. The outward actions which he approved might appear contradictory but really have a consistency on a level not understood by his opponents. He circumcised Timothy, but refused to circumcise Titus. He refused the demand that Gentiles should be subject to the law, but did not hesitate to observe temple services and Jewish rites himself. Words and acts such as these provided the grounds for charges of inconsistency which were made in bitter disparagement of his work.

Paul had declared the exclusiveness and intolerance of God's gospel in terms that could not be made stronger (verses 8,9). In verse 10 he asks, "For do I now 'persuade men', or God? or do I seek to 'please men'? for if I yet pleased men, I should not be the servant of Christ".

There was nothing in the words he has just penned that lent support to the charge that he was just a "man pleaser", trimming and accommodating the gospel message. An ellipsis is involved in the first question, the thought being supplied in some way such as, "Or, am I concerned about God?" He could please men and satisfy the Jewish traducers by teaching the need for observing the law and accepting the rite of circumcision. In fact, the hatred he endured from the Jews belied the charge against him: but, says Paul (RV), "If I were still pleasing men"—if he were complying with the wishes of the Jews—then he would not be *Christ's* servant, or slave. He would, in fact, have surrendered to a servitude to men. But he bore the marks which proved him to be Christ's slave. The effects of persecutions which had been witnessed by the Galatians of Lystra and Derbe were so many brandings in his flesh that showed he belonged to Christ. The Galatians ought not to be in doubt about that.

### The Gospel's Divine Origin

If then Paul's sincerity was beyond dispute, was he nevertheless mistaken ? What was the basis of his teaching ? What his authority? To this he turns in the following words: "But I certify you, brethren, that the gospel which was preached of me is not after man. For I neither received it of man, neither was I taught it, but by the revelation of Jesus Christ" (verses 11,12).

"Not after man" indicates that it was not humanly devised; it was not the product of men's thoughts and scheming. In its form and character his message bore the mark of a higher origin and it had the authority that belonged to its divine source. Paul amplifies his meaning: he had not received it of men, neither had he been taught it by men. That is, neither had the message come from any man, nor had any man explained its significance to Paul. In every way a human

25

channel is excluded. On the contrary, he had received it "by the revelation of Jesus Christ". By this phrase we must understand that Jesus was the one who made the revelation, and not that Jesus was the subject of the revelation, made to Paul. In other words, his knowledge of the gospel, his message that he proclaimed, had the personal authority of Jesus. When and how the gospel was thus given in fulness to Paul we may not be able to determine with certainty. We know that he had a unique experience on the way to Damascus. The prophets had received the word of the Lord by dream, by oracle, by angelic communication. Even John, the beloved disciple, had not the revelation of Jesus Christ direct from his Master, but by the angel through whom Jesus Christ had sent and signified it. But Paul had met Jesus, and had "seen that Just One, and had heard a voice from his mouth". When this beginning of a revelation by Jesus Christ was supplemented we may not know. Paul refers to visions and revelations of the Lord which he had fourteen years before he wrote the letters to Corinth. This must refer to a time some five years after his conversion. But whatever further communication Paul had, the fact that Jesus had met him, had spoken to him and given him his commission, was in itself sufficient to mark him out as being in an exceptional position.

Our knowledge of the means whereby divine ideas can be implanted in a man's mind and so become his and yet not his, is very small. In the utterances of the prophets were some matters they themselves had to examine to reach the meaning of their own words. In Paul's case, however, the message preached was not only a declaration of God's grace, but a reasoned testimony incorporating the witness of the earlier revelation in the Old Testament. Paul's message must not only have been communicated to him in some way, but must have also been built up into his own consciousness so that it became his own mode of thinking. In his own case this involved considerable unlearning of things taught him by the rabbis, and in that process he found that one-time stumbling blocks to faith became steps by which he climbed upwards to clearer vision and greater faith.

PAUL'S GOSPEL NOT DERIVED FROM HIS EARLIER LIFE (1:13,14)

THE declaration that Paul's early life had contributed nothing to his present knowledge throws into greater relief the fact that his understanding of God's plan was by revelation. Absent indeed from his early outlook had been any seeds of development which would grow into Christian faith—far otherwise. The Galatians knew his story—his course of life as a bitter enemy and persecutor of the Christians, and his efforts to destroy their faith from the earth. That was the outcome of his earlier faith; and the intensity of his opposition to Jesus and his followers was proportionate to his outstanding Jewish zeal. He had been brought up in an exclusive Jewish home, being as he claimed a Hebrew sprung from Hebrews; he had graduated in the leading college of their nation, had sat at the feet of their greatest teacher. He had been an apt pupil, outshining his fellow-students in his zeal and earnestness and his application to the study of the law. "I profited", he says, "in the Jews' religion above many my equals in mine own nation, being more exceedingly zealous of the traditions of my fathers" (verse 14). The traditional teaching of the Jews had been his very life; it led him to resist the message of Christians. It was clear therefore that his present faith and message could not have sprung from his earlier belief.

PAUL'S GOSPEL NOT RECEIVED FROM OTHER TEACHERS
(1:15–17)

IN verse 12 Paul had asserted that he had not received his message of men, or been taught it by men. He had shown by the reference to his earlier way of life that the Christian message could not have sprung from his old beliefs. He must complete the proof of its divine origin by showing also that he had not been instructed by men. To do this it was necessary to recount his contacts with those who, in the view of Paul's enemies, might have been his teachers. He must begin, therefore, with his conversion. When that occurred, he says, although he was commissioned then to preach, he did not seek an interview with the older apostles but at first led a secluded life. It will be well to quote his words:

"But when it pleased God, who separated me from my mother's womb, and called me by his grace, to reveal his Son in me, that I might preach him among the heathen; immediately I conferred not with flesh and blood: neither went I up to Jerusalem to them which were apostles before me; but I went into Arabia, and returned again unto Damascus." (verses 15–17)

Paul was a Pharisee, a "separated" one as the name indicates. He had then thought that he had found the ideal, and knew the goal of life; he had reached a spiritual pinnacle in the Pharisees' way of life. He now found there had been another "separation" going on unknown to him, to which his

27

human Pharisaism contributed nothing but shame and humiliation. (That was indeed something, in this sense: the product of Pharisaism was seen by Paul to be so alien to God's way that the new and living way in Christ was seen in greater contrast; and Paul's zealous efforts of old only made him realise how great can be man's foolishness and how much he needs God's mercy.)

As Paul looked back on his life he could trace the divine hand in the circumstances that had gone to the shaping of his life, even from the earliest days. "From my mother's womb" may indicate that even before his birth he was foreknown and chosen for the work he had to do. The peculiar combination of influences that made the preaching of the gospel possible in the first century as at no other time before or since had all played their part in Paul's own development and qualification for the task God had for him to do. Roman, Greek and Jew—all had contributed. His citizenship, his speech and his religion—the dominant factors in the man's making—were drawn from the outstanding factors of first century life. These were the external influences whose interaction made Paul the persecutor, and which—when something more important than any of the three was added—made Paul the apostle. That something Paul describes when he says he was "called by his grace". The "call" of Paul was the most potent of all influences, all the others from the time of his conversion being made contributory to the "new man", being used by that "new "man" to subserve the great purpose he had thenceforward to perform.

That purpose for which God had prepared Saul is defined as God's pleasure "to reveal his Son in me that I might preach him among the Gentiles". In verse 12 he had spoken of "the revelation of Jesus Christ"—a revelation that came from Jesus Christ. The effect of that revelation was the formation in Paul of a likeness to the Son of God, defined by himself as "Christ in me". He was thus fitted to preach Christ and reveal Christ to others. The man and the message were in harmony. He could therefore write to the Thessalonians:

"Ye know what manner of men we were among you for your sake. And ye became followers of us and of the Lord." (1 Thessalonians 1:5,6)

—and to Timothy:

"And I thank Christ Jesus our Lord, who hath enabled me, for that he counted me faithful, putting me into the ministry; who was before a blasphemer, and a persecutor, and injurious: but I obtained mercy, because I did it ignorantly in unbelief. And the grace of our Lord was exceeding abundant with faith and love which is in Christ Jesus. This is a faithful saying, and worthy of all acceptation, that Christ Jesus came into the world to save sinners; of whom I am chief. Howbeit for this cause I obtained mercy, that in me first Jesus Christ might shew forth all long suffering, for a pattern to them which should hereafter believe on him to life everlasting." (1 Timothy 1:12–16)

When God interfered in Paul's life in the direct fashion that only Paul among the apostles experienced (unless there was some corresponding experience in Peter's life to which Jesus refers when he says, "Flesh and blood hath not revealed this unto thee, but my Father which is in heaven"), at once Paul went to Arabia. There was no conference with others and no meeting with the other apostles at Jerusalem.

Nothing can be said with certainty about what place the Apostle denotes by Arabia. In 4:25 he refers to Sinai in Arabia, and it is therefore difficult to exclude the peninsula of Sinai from the word Arabia as he uses it in 1:17. It seems to be established that the name included regions quite near to Damascus, and even for a period that city itself. But it would not be natural when Paul was there immediately after his conversion to speak of going to Arabia if Damascus were part of it. He could, however, say he went into Arabia and yet not travel far from the city of Damascus. But wherever he sojourned his language would imply that the three years interval before he went to Jerusalem was not spent in either preaching or discussing his gospel with other leaders. It was spent in habituating his mind to the new understanding of God and His ways, guided by revelation from the Lord.

## PAUL'S FIRST VISIT TO JERUSALEM (1:18–20)

ALL who have studied the life of the Apostle Paul know that there has been much controversy concerning the identification of Paul's visits to Jerusalem as recorded in Acts and Galatians. Many factors have to be taken into account. The revival of the idea that the Galatians to whom the epistle was penned are the Churches of the four towns where Paul preached on his first journey, has led to the view that Galatians was written earlier than had been for long believed. The powerful advocacy of Sir Wm. Ramsay and two or three other scholars has led to a growing acceptance of the South Galatian theory, and with it a readjustment has taken place not only of the date when the letter was written, but also of the cross-references in Acts and the epistle.

We do not intend to attempt any discussion of the reasons put forward on either side of the controversy. We shall follow the epistle and give the connections with Acts which we believe to be the best founded and which make clearest the apostle's argument and also the course of history in early apostolic times.

Paul had declared that, contrary to the charges made by his opponents, the gospel he preached had not been received from men, nor yet taught by men. To establish the fact that no man had instructed him in the gospel, he must give the true facts concerning his contacts with the older apostles. The Judaizers would certainly make the most of any circumstances that would tend to disparage Paul. Something which called for correction must have been said about his first visit to Jerusalem and the object of the visit. Only this can explain the statement so solemnly made on oath that what he narrated was the truth. "Now the things which I write unto you, behold, before God, I lie not" (1:20).

Paul mentions two visits to Jerusalem between which was an interval spent in Syria and Cilicia. He also describes a third meeting with an apostle which took place at Antioch. The first visit is dated three years after his conversion—a period of time which may not have been more than two years. Part of this period he had spent in Arabia. He "went up", Paul explained, "to see Peter" with whom he abode fifteen days. There was no conference with other apostles—Paul saw none of them, only James the Lord's brother, who, though not an apostle in the restricted sense, had an important place in the councils of the Church in Jerusalem.

He went to *see* Peter: or, as the RV, "to visit" him. The word Paul uses describes such a visit as when people go to "view" a place, to see its buildings. Peter was well known as the foremost of the apostles, and it was quite a natural thing that Paul should wish to "become acquainted with" (RV marg.) him. But this very meaning of the word excludes the notion of any consultation for instruction and information.

### The Intervention of Barnabas

The record in Acts shows that so far from Paul being welcomed as a desirable pupil, he was at first avoided. Luke's account reads:

> "And when Saul was come to Jerusalem, he assayed to join himself to the disciples: but they were all afraid of

him, and believed not that he was a disciple. But Barnabas took him, and brought him to the apostles, and declared unto them how he had seen the Lord in the way, and that he had spoken to him, and how he had preached boldly at Damascus in the name of Jesus. And he was with them coming in and going out at Jerusalem. And he spake boldly in the name of the Lord Jesus, and disputed against the Grecians: but they went about to slay him. Which when the brethren knew, they brought him down to Cæsarea, and sent him forth to Tarsus." (Acts 9:26–30)

This account gives us the external features of the visit. It required the warmhearted, generous sponsoring of Barnabas to make Paul acceptable to the church. Barnabas took Paul "to the apostles". This is not a contradiction with Galatians, for the term does not define the individual men but the holders of the office, and in being introduced to James he was thus made known to a representative of the apostles. The other apostles would probably be on preaching journeys.

We are left to conjecture why the labours of Paul were limited to the Grecians. He would visit the synagogues of the Diaspora, where Greek-speaking Jews and Gentile proselytes assembled. He did what Stephen had done before, and he met the same opposition that had befallen Stephen. We have another record of this visit from Paul's own account of his conversion in Acts 22. He there tells of a visit to the temple, when, while praying, he received a communication from the Lord: "Make haste to get thee quickly out of Jerusalem: for they will not receive thy testimony concerning me". Paul thought that the very fact that he had been a persecutor, but was now a preacher of that he had sought to destroy, would commend his message. So he argued when told to leave the city; but the command was repeated in more peremptory terms: "Depart: for I will send thee far hence unto the Gentiles".

If the rumours of the plots to slay Paul had reached his ears, this message would show what action he must follow. Accordingly he was conducted by brethren to Cæsarea and thence to Tarsus.

The statement Paul makes in the Galatians seems simple and withal apparently of little moment. Yet Paul solemnly affirms its truth, and it must therefore have had great value in his defence. Its importance doubtless lay in the correction of some false statements which had been circulated by his enemies about the visit, to which a simple and emphatic statement that it was to become acquainted with Peter was a sufficient refutation. What his enemies said can only be a matter of surmise.

IN SYRIA AND CILICIA (1:21–24)

OF the interval between the first and second visits to the Holy City, the only information we have is in these verses. The emphatic "afterwards" which introduces the statement shows it to be part of a number of items all bearing upon the absence of human authority in the establishing of Paul's apostleship. "Afterwards", he says, "I came into the regions of Syria and Cilicia; and was unknown by face unto the churches of Judea which were in Christ: but they had heard only, That he which persecuted us in times past now preacheth the faith which once he destroyed. And they glorified God in me." The coincidence with Acts is found in the fact that at the end of the nine years so spent, Barnabas, needing Paul for the work which was growing in Antioch in Syria, went to Tarsus "to *seek* Saul" (Acts 11:25). He had to seek him: his precise whereabouts would be unknown, for he was spending his time preaching. His activities were indeed known. The Judean churches heard that the erstwhile persecutor was busily preaching that faith he once destroyed.

Paul speaks of being unknown by face to the churches of Judea. This has been thought to conflict with the record in Acts, but such a conflict only exists when the difference is not noticed between the church in Jerusalem and the churches in Judea. On the visit Paul only met the brethren in the capital city; he was unknown to any others throughout the province.

The fact that this period was spent in preaching so fruitfully that the fame of it reached Judea, has a bearing upon Paul's case. His commission to preach did not begin with the separation of himself and Barnabas to go on a preaching tour. That was for a new task, marking a fresh development of the work. The commission came with the announcement at the time of his conversion that he was "a chosen vessel", and with this his preaching began. It was confirmed when he had the vision in the Temple at his first visit by the instruction to leave Jerusalem and go to the Gentiles.

So much was his work approved that the news of it caused the churches of Judea to glorify God in Paul.

PAUL'S SECOND VISIT TO JERUSALEM (2:1–10)

THOSE writers who identify the visit to Jerusalem described in these verses with the Council of Acts 15 are compelled to say that for some reason Paul omits in Galatians any reference to the visit for carrying relief described in Acts 11:30. For Paul to vindicate his independence of the other apostles for the gospel he preached, it would seem to be essential, however, that he should name every visit *prior* to his first visit to Galatia. To do otherwise would lay himself open to the charge of having left out of his defence the very visit when the apostles authorised him to preach and instructed him in his message. His vindication would not be complete with such an omission: every contact with the other apostles therefore must be mentioned. This consideration gives great probability, if not certainty, to the identification of Galatians 2:1–10 with Acts 11:30. The fourteenth year must then be reckoned from Paul's conversion, and not from the first visit to Jerusalem of Galatians 1:18.

It is important to remember that in a statement such as this defence there is a background of thought, of charge, of contention, all of which is not known to a present reader but which was familiar to the first readers. Expressions which are ambiguous to us were clear to the Galatians; allusions which we may miss were significant to them. And in comparing the epistle with Acts we must remember that Luke's history was written for a purpose other than the vindication of Paul against the attack of his Jewish traducers; therefore some filling in of detail belongs to the particular purpose each had in writing of the visit. The details differ in keeping with the particular purpose in the story.

One strong objection to the generally accepted identification of Galatians 2:1–10 with the council of Acts 15 is that at that Council Paul did receive decrees which embodied its decision. But Paul omits any reference to that matter in Galatians 2:1–10, and this omission would be fatal to his claim of truthfulness (1:20) if the visit he describes was to the council. But if Paul's Galatian churches are those evangelised on the first journey, then the council had not occurred at the time and the authentication of the message Paul had given them was independent of it. In fact, Paul took the decrees of the council to Galatia on the second visit, and the victory against the Judaizers was then won. But if we date the Galatian letter before the council—which is more probable— we then see that Paul is fighting the battle in the epistle which was also fought in the council. In both the issue is decided against the teaching that the law was binding upon the Christians.

## Paul's Second Visit

We now consider Paul's account of his second visit to Jerusalem in more detail. He went up with Barnabas, and Titus went with them. The same verb, "taking", is used in in Acts 12:25 of John Mark, and signifies that Mark went as an assistant. So with Titus. The visit being for relief, there would have to be considerable organisation and transport. Since famine conditions prevailed, Paul and Barnabas would have to purchase food elsewhere and take it to Jerusalem. We get a wrong picture if we think of them taking money which could be spent in Jerusalem. On such a work of collecting food an assistant would be desirable, and the ability which Titus showed on later occasions would suggest that the choice was a wise one. Acts tells us that the relief was sent by "the hands of Barnabas and Saul" (Acts 11:30).

The visit was by revelation. If we depended on the epistle alone we might reasonably infer that the revelation was given to Paul which led him to make the visit. But Acts tells us the prophecy of Agabus of the coming famine was the revelation. This was probably well known, but in any case the important point in Paul's case is that he did not of his own initiative go to seek the advice or help of the apostles in Jerusalem. While there, however, he did lay before them (the Church) the gospel which he preached, and then he had private communication with three apostles. His reason for this private interview he states: he did not want the gospel he was already preaching to be in vain. This would have been the case if there had not been agreement about Paul's work. In the joining of Jew and Gentile in one church there were all the factors for strife and trouble. If there had been a Jewish Christian Church and a Gentile Christian Church, it would have been fatal to that unity of all redeemed in Christ. Paul therefore wished them to know of his work and sphere of labour, and the results of his preaching.

When Paul refers to the three as "them which were of rep-utation" and those "who seemed to be somewhat" (verses 2 and 6), we must not regard his language as disparaging. Such a construction would be out of keeping with Paul's friendly attitude to those who were apostles before him and also to the friendly spirit which evidently pervaded the interview. If the Judaizers had used the words concerning the older apos-tles in disparagement of Paul, we have a reason for Paul's reference. He says that when he met those who were of repute it was not to be instructed by them, but to enter into a contract concerning the division of the labour in the gospel between the two parties.

The assistant Titus, being a Greek, would naturally attract attention, and it is clear that he was the cause of some discussion. Paul says that false brethren were the leaders of it. Paul's language is compressed and his grammatical construction broken: but certain clear impressions emerge. The Judaizers did not like Titus being present, and instigated some men to make investigations. This was done under cover of a pretended friendship. An agitation began that Titus ought to be circumcised, but Paul resisted this from the first hint of it. To have yielded to such a course would have destroyed the liberty in Christ and imposed the bondage of the law upon Christians. The conflicting views which were thus made apparent made it desirable that Paul should see the three leaders—but there was no debate with them, no difference of opinion, but perfect harmony and agreement.

An interpretation that makes the operative word *compelled*, as though Paul agreed for the sake of peace that Titus should be circumcised, but voluntarily and not under compulsion, does not fit the tenor of the argument. Had such happened Paul's case would have needed stating in a very different way and with very different reasons for the action. Paul was shocked at the duplicity of the men who proposed that Titus should be circumcised—they had pretended friendship with ulterior motives. Not for a second could Paul have agreed that Titus should submit to the rite. A concession under such circumstances would have been fatal.

In fact—and Paul reverts to the meeting with the three elder apostles (verse 6)—the interview added nothing to Paul. The Three had no authority in Paul's case and gave him no instruction or information. On the contrary, it was Paul who stated the case for Gentile acceptance without the law; and since the divine approval of Paul's teaching was evident, as also that Paul's ministry was as effectual among the Gentiles as Peter's was amongst Jews, the Three gave Paul the right hand of fellowship. The division of work was agreed upon—Paul's labour was among Gentiles, theirs among the Jews. Only one proposal was made—that Paul should remember the poor. This was an apposite suggestion, for Paul was then in Jerusalem on such an errand.

The meeting of the five men in Jerusalem, mentioned only in this epistle, and that merely as part of a defence of Paul's own apostleship, was yet surely one of the most important ever held. The evident harmony that prevailed indicates the fine spirit of loyalty to God's instruction which was a moving force in the spread of Christianity. There was no petty jealousy; no rivalry of schools of thought. There was no Paulinism opposed to the teaching of the older apostles such as some modern critical theories have postulated with consequent destructive speculations concerning the early history of Christianity and the genuineness of the writings which were produced in the first generation. God's will was recognised by all; the loyal response opened the gates wide to full and free activity among all men.

## PAUL AND PETER AT ANTIOCH (2:11–21)

WHEN did the meeting between the two great apostles, which Paul describes, take place? It cannot be determined with anything approaching certainty, and suggestions are influenced by the view held concerning the time when the Galatian letter was written. If we put the letter before the second missionary journey the idea follows naturally that Peter visited Antioch at some time during the progress of the work there in which Barnabas and Paul were engaged as recorded in Acts 14:27,28. It may be that on his release from prison the "other place" to which Peter went (Acts 12:17) was Antioch. About that time we know the circumstances existed which are mentioned in Galatians 2. Paul and Barnabas were present, and at that time men from Jerusalem visited Antioch. In Acts 15:1 we read "certain men which came down from Judea taught the brethren, and said, Except ye be circumcised after the manner of Moses, ye cannot be saved", while Paul spoke of "certain that came from James" through whose influence Peter and Barnabas dissembled. It may be, however, that the visit of the brethren from James was even earlier than Acts 15:1.

The effects of the agitation by the visitors from Judea were disturbing. Before their advent the harmony between Jewish and Gentile believers had been greatly encouraged by the free mixing with Gentiles of leading brethren like Peter and Barnabas. They shared the same meals as the Gentiles, and it was recognised that there was complete freedom from the Mosaic law. Then the visitors arrived and declared the necessity of circumcision for salvation. In the absence of the observance of the rite, the Jewish visitors would not acknowledge the Gentile converts as Christians. So assertive were they that the old pliability of Peter overcame his better judgement, and he ceased to share the common meal with the Gentiles.

If Peter was being informed by the messengers from James that Herod's death by divine judgement had removed the danger from which he had fled, and that he was needed in Jerusalem, we might imagine Peter yielding to the argument that he could not return to Jerusalem if he were ceremonially defiled by contact with Gentiles. Feeling the work in Jerusalem would be thus imperilled, we might suppose, he capitulated. Such an interpretation may be the correct one — it is more generous, and perhaps more just, to Peter than many explanations. But even so, his action undermined the basic principle of God's dealing with men. Other Jews followed his example, and even Barnabas was caught up in the flood.

Paul saw that the whole work among the Gentiles was in jeopardy. The practice of Peter in eating freely with Gentiles was a logical consequence of a faith in Christ shared alike by Jew and Gentile. To revert to the old Jewish way of life virtually rejected the gospel of Christ and reasserted the necessary observance of law as a condition of salvation. The action of Peter has had effects in later history in addition to the immediate consequences in the ecclesia of Antioch. In the second century the episode caused much bitter disputation; and in the nineteenth century a theory of early church history which considerably influenced critical views perverted the facts by presuming a permanent conflict between the views of Peter and Paul. Peter's course of action before the Judaizers appeared was in perfect harmony with Paul: his lapse was temporary, and harmony was restored both doctrinally and personally. Peter later speaks of Paul as the "beloved brother Paul". Both Peter and Paul recognised that the truth of the gospel was of greater moment than the men who proclaimed it, and a lapse was something to be deplored, and its correction a ground of thankfulness.

## The Need for the Rebuke

Paul's piercing logic and stern sense of duty to the gospel made inevitable the resistance to Peter. The circumstances did not admit of private expostulation: the freedom of the gospel had been publicly assailed by Peter's conduct and public action was called for. "When I saw that they walked not uprightly according to the truth of the gospel, I said unto Peter before them all, If thou, being a Jew, livest after the manner of Gentiles, and not as do the Jews, why compellest thou the Gentiles to live as do the Jews?" (verse 14). This defence of the gospel to Peter as recounted by Paul passes at some point to a statement to the Galatians. It still continues to describe Paul's attitude to the issue in question, but in the course of the narrative in the letter Paul in thought has left Peter and is with the Galatians and is stating his case to them. Where the transition is none can say: there are advocates of making the division at verse 15, in verse 16, and between 18 and 19. Certain it is that the transition occurs, and while the theme continues and the speaker is the same, the listeners have changed.

But what a revelation is this statement of the man Paul! He cannot be understood by anyone who has not tried to follow his intense and moving words as he describes from the innermost recesses of his being his convictions concerning Christ. He never loses his logical presentation of his thought, but it is charged with deepest feeling and emotion. We will try to follow his thought and also to comprehend his feeling. "We", Paul continued to Peter—and the "we" means Peter and Paul—"we who are Jews by nature and not sinners of the Gentiles ..." (verse 15). The Jew is here speaking—a Jew with all the pride of race and zeal for religion that marked the best of them—and the Jew speaking is both Paul the scholar and rabbi, and Peter the blunt, homely, but earnest fisherman. The Gentiles were a lesser breed without the law; they were sinners. Gentiles had no pretensions to righteousness: without God and without the restraining influence of law, their general life was only too accurately described by Paul in Romans 1. When such came to a knowledge of the Holy One of Israel and of His righteous law, it was only too evident they were sinners. But both Paul and Peter had found that they too were sinners in God's sight; and even if they had escaped the grosser sins of the Gentiles, they had nevertheless by their education in the law acquired a clearer view of the sinfulness of sin and of man's failure before God. Their consciousness of sin was not less but greater than the Gentiles. Experience had taught them that a man is not justified by works of law. Paul gave expression to a universal fact when he declared that when the law came into his life he became aware of a contrary impulse in himself ready to assert itself. This impulse he calls sin; and he became aware of its power when the law's prohibitions were understood by him. Sin sprang to life—it was there but dormant, only waiting the assertion of righteous law to be awakened into a vigour which would never abate till life itself was spent. Such experience to a soul that knew God to be real, led to a recognition that death must inevitably be the result. Bluntly, Paul declares, "and I died" (Romans 7:9).

If law had the effect of stirring up the antagonism of the flesh it is clear that justification could not be by law—for justification is a pronouncement of righteousness, a declaration that a man is righteous. What the law inevitably did was to convict a man of being a sinner.

Into the life of Peter, Paul and all Jewish believers had come the light of salvation. While the light more certainly than law made clear the sinfulness of man, it yet showed the way to life in Christ Jesus. By faith in him a man was justified, was pronounced righteous; for in response to faith in what had been accomplished in Jesus Christ, God forgave a man his sins. What a man could not be by law he could become by faith; he could stand before God a forgiven man and so be reckoned a righteous man.

## The Relief from Burden

The glad relief from the law's burden and the joy of freedom in Christ had been the experience of both apostles. Both had believed on Christ: they had rested on him in the conviction that justification could not be found elsewhere at all.

Scripture itself asserted what experience had taught: "By the works of the law shall no flesh be justified". David had pleaded, "Enter not into judgment with thy servant; for in thy sight shall no man living be justified" (Psalm 143:2). The Psalm must have had a firm place in Paul's thought, for in Romans 3 he closes his survey of the whole world's need of God's mercy by a final word on even the Jews' desperate poverty of righteousness:

"Now we know that what things soever the law saith, it saith to them who are under the law: that every mouth may be stopped, and all the world may become guilty before God. Therefore by the deeds of the law there shall no flesh be justified in his sight: for by the law is the knowledge of sin." (Romans 3:19,20)

There were many subtle arguments to be met from Jewish opponents. The gospel did not come into the world at a time of mental stagnation, even if it was a time of moral bankruptcy. Jew and Gentile resisted Christian teaching by human reasonings. Nowhere is the deceitfulness of sin more clearly shown than in the "rationalising" thought by which sin is excused and persistence in it justified. "Let us continue in sin that grace may abound" was a brazen argument for living in sin that demanded for answer the emphatic "God forbid". So with the attempt to make Christ the cause of sin. It was perversely declared that if the gospel of Christ made a man more conscious of sin, so that he felt himself as the result to be a worse sinner, then Christ must be a promoter of sin. The argument is self-condemned and is repudiated sternly: "God forbid". It is the peculiar characteristic of sin that it blinds the sinner to the real evil of sin. Sin deceives, but that which exposes sin and reveals its true character as sin, must in its very nature be contrary to sin.

In verse 18, Paul states in his own person the position of others—Peter, Barnabas, and the Galatians who had acted in the same way. He puts hypothetically for himself what in fact others were doing. This must be recognised to understand Paul's words; and with its recognition we become aware that we are leaving Peter and Antioch and are in the presence of the defaulting Galatians. "If I build again, or if Peter or Barnabas or you build again, the things I or you once destroyed, I and you prove ourselves to be transgressors." What had they destroyed? They had cast out the notion that life could be by law—that by law's works they could be justified. And now to go back to law was to seek for their justification from that which their whole experience had shown to be a "minister of condemnation". This was to fly in the face of God's own decree, and His purpose in the law, and therefore made them transgressors.

### Paul's Experience

The "for" which introduces verse 19 shows that the statement introduced by it is the explanation and demonstration of what Paul meant by his words in verse 18, "I make myself a transgressor". The "for" introduces the most moving piece of spiritual biography ever penned: in it the intensity of the apostle's struggle with himself is revealed, and the completeness of his surrender to Christ is set forth. Few comprehended Christ as Paul did, for the very depth of his nature and the brilliance of his intellect were the ground of his bitter opposition and then the basis of his complete devotion as Christ's slave. No more illustrious captive ever marked the triumphal progress of God's Son. His humiliation was complete; his surrender was absolute. With the utter relentlessness of straight thinking he saw how completely wrong he had been and therefore how great was God's grace in Christ which gave him life and hope.

"For I through the law am dead to the law, that I might live unto God" (verse 19). His experience of law—and his very earnestness and devotion to the law as a Pharisee made his experience more complete—had shown that it could not justify; that that was beyond its power. On the contrary, it condemned to death. As a source of salvation the law was of no avail. Whether therefore because it condemned him to death, or because by it he could never get life, Paul died to the law. He passed from its jurisdiction over him when he entered the service of Christ, freed from its effects and its demands. As he says in his letter to the Romans:

"Wherefore, my brethren, ye also are become dead to the law by the body of Christ ... For when we were in the flesh the motions of sins, which were by the law, did work in our members to bring forth fruit unto death. But now we are delivered from the law, that being dead wherein we were held; that we should serve in newness of spirit, and not in the oldness of the letter." (Romans 7:4–6)

That service in newness of spirit is "living unto God". The antithesis of death and life expresses Paul's personal relationship to law and to God. He strove to live under the law and he died to it; he passed by that death into a new service which was in fact life in God's sight. The death and the life are next described in terms which bring these things, and Paul who experienced them, into relationship to Christ.

"I am crucified with Christ: nevertheless I live; yet not I, but Christ liveth in me: and the life which I now live in the flesh I live by the faith of the Son of God, who loved me, and gave himself for me" (verse 20). The words are figurative—so much so to most people that the stark significance of the figure is lost on them. There is an ecclesiastical glamour about the cross; an emotional, sentimental feeling that has robbed crucifixion of its ugliness and shame. But Paul knew too much of what crucifixion meant as a horrible mode of death to sentimentalise about it. He knew also of the shame with which a Jew thought of a man who claimed to be his Messiah coming to such an end. "The scandal of the cross" was a deep-seated resentment of the very idea that a man who so met his death should be thought of at all as Israel's Messiah; the cross was a final proof that Jesus was an impostor.

Paul was closely associated with the ruling body of Israel. Probably he was a member of the Sanhedrin. It would seem reasonable to think that he would be in Jerusalem at some time during Christ's ministry and would be acquainted with the reports sent in by the emissaries of the rulers concerning Jesus. Even if not actually in Jerusalem at the close of the ministry he must have been familiar with the attitude of the authorities to Jesus. He would hear with approval that Jesus had been put to death. The man who later watched the death of Stephen when the witnesses, to free their arms to throw the stones, laid their garments at his feet, had in thought stood and watched with approval the death of Jesus. In thought he, too, had derided him, scoffed at him, and felt that it was a just end.

## Jesus no Impostor

Then Paul learned, not by hearsay or report, but by an actual meeting with Jesus that permitted of no mistake, that the man he thought was an impostor was a divine reality; the man he thought to be dead was alive. And the whole theory of Paul's life which was based on the idea that Jesus was dead, itself crumbled into dust when he met the living Christ. He was not dead; he was alive. That meant that Paul had to reshape his mental and spiritual life in keeping with that fact. Jesus was no impostor: he was true: it was Paul who was wrong. And as he was wrong in his theory of Jesus, so his action in persecuting the followers of Jesus was a perpetuation of the sin which had been done by the nation in rejecting and crucifying Jesus. Paul had continued the crucifixion in slaying the followers, for had not the glorified Jesus charged Paul with persecuting *him*: "Why persecutest thou me?"

Paul had been tragically wrong, but he was not dishonest. He saw the wrong, made no attempt to hide it, but applied himself to see the truth and to live in it. He must now know what the divine will had been in the crucifixion of Jesus, for that it was the divine will was clear, for Jesus was justified by God in being raised from death. As he said in the opening words of this Galatian letter: "Christ gave himself for our sins ... according to the will of God and our Father."

When Paul passes in his thought away from Peter to the Galatians, he does so because what he said to Peter he had previously said to the Galatians. He is re-stating the message he had given them when he first preached to them. They would recognise this at once: but the message Paul had given them was none other than the message he insisted upon when Peter was "to be blamed" and which message Peter had acknowledged to be true in accepting Paul's reproof. The recital, then, of this meeting with Peter has a real bearing upon Paul's argument in his defence. He received nothing from others: the apostles had accepted his divine commission that he should preach to Gentiles: but it was Peter who had faltered, and it was Paul who had stood firm in the defence of the true gospel.

When we perceive this, we can fill in the details of Paul's message to the Galatians. "Christ had been placarded before them" (Galatians 3:1), and the reason for his death had been explained. The letter to the Romans is Paul's own statement of what he therein describes as "my gospel". In that gospel he shows the universal failure of man to attain to righteousness. All have sinned and all deserve the wages of sin, which is death. All are dying as members of a race that are descendants of the "one man" through whom sin entered the world and death by sin, and so death passed upon all men, for that all have sinned. Paul showed that God had set forth Jesus to declare His righteousness that God might be just and the justifier of them that believe. Jesus had declared God's righteousness when, as a member of a death-stricken race, he voluntarily laid down his life. In his death Jesus "died unto sin" in that he came under death's dominion because sin had brought all the race under death's thrall. In the willing submission to crucifixion Jesus had shown that the nature in which sin inhered, but which had never been allowed to overcome him, was unfitted to live and lay rightly under divine sentence. The prince of this world (sin) was judged and condemned in the flesh of sin so that he could be a sacrifice for sin, a sin-offering. All had been done that God might provide a just basis upon which He could forgive sin.

## The Sin Offering

Where the law worked wrath in that it brought a man under the penalty of broken law, the crucifixion of Jesus was an expression of God's love in providing the way for the exercise of His mercy. "God commendeth his love toward us in that while we were yet sinners, Christ died for us" (Romans 5:8). It also is an expression of the love of Christ: as Paul says,

> "The love of Christ constraineth us; because we thus judge, that if one died for all, then were all dead: and that he died for all, that they which live should not henceforth live unto themselves, but unto him which died for them, and rose again." (2 Corinthians 5:14,15)

But the connection between a sinner and Christ the sin-offering was to be found in the voluntary identifying of the sinner with the Saviour. In baptism a man is "buried with Christ" and "risen with him". In that act "our old man is crucified with Christ". This act of identification is seen by Paul in all the vividness of an actual association with Jesus on the cross. Instead of standing with the ring of jeering spectators, Paul crosses over to the crucified. He endorses the crucified's action in being there, in laying down his life, and in laying it down in that way. He joins Christ on the cross, and dies with him. In this way Paul endorses the divine principles exhibited in that death of Jesus.

43

Jesus the crucified and the buried was, however, Jesus the raised to unending life. As Paul shares his death, he shares the new life toward God made possible in Christ. So he says, "I live": but at once, lest that should appear to claim any personal quality of Paul's own, he adds "Yet not I, but Christ liveth in me". That does not mean that Paul as a personality has ceased to be; it means that Paul in Christ is empowered to live a life in which Christ is seen in Paul's life. For the sacrifice of Christ is not only expiatory, is not only a means for God's mercy to forgive sins, but the sacrifice of Christ is a motive power to holiness; in Paul's words: "The life which I now live in the flesh I live by the faith of the Son of God, who loved me and gave himself for me." Paul the sensitive soul so conscious of sin; Paul the persecutor of Christ's followers, saw in Christ's death a revelation of Christ's love for that same Paul. The crucifixion was not just a theological term but a real factor in Paul's life toward God.

He saw in it all God's grace. To seek another way of life is to frustrate that divine way, to frustrate God's grace. That way God had chosen was the only possible way; for if righteousness had been by another way, by law, then Christ died for nought: under the scheme of law his death was unnecessary—and if men turned to law they acted as if that were the fact.

When we have tried to follow Paul's vivid figure of identification with Christ crucified and the implication of it, we can understand Paul's horror of defection from Christ. That horror is expressed in the reverse figure. If a man who has known the truth in Jesus turns away, he denies that truth and in action declares Jesus to be the impostor the Jew thought him to be. His action then endorses the Jew's act of crucifying Jesus. Paul says that if a man has had unmistakable evidence of truth and then repudiates it, "he crucifies to himself the Son of God afresh" (Hebrews 6:6). If to share Christ's crucifixion is to share his salvation, to crucify him is to deserve the fate of his crucifiers and of all who spurn the love of God and the love of Christ—the Christ who despised the shame of the cross that men might live.

# SECTION 3

## PAUL'S GOSPEL: FAITH SUPERIOR TO LAW
### AN APPEAL TO EXPERIENCE (3:1–6)

IF Christ had not died in vain, if, in other words, his death was essential (2:21)—and none of Paul's readers would dispute that his death was a fact and was the essential factor in God's plan for their salvation—then anything that took them away from Christ took them away from God and His redemption. To follow any course which had that result was folly.

It was, therefore, a true description when Paul addressed them as "foolish Galatians". The use of the geographical term may also suggest that they were not living up to the standard about which they had rather prided themselves. By Galatia Paul meant the Roman province of Galatia, and the four Galatian towns were closely bound up with imperial administration. The spirit of the towns partook of that pride of place and culture generally found in Greco-Roman cities—a pride in progress and enlightenment. For *such* people to be guilty of the folly of turning from God's grace suggested that something had bewitched them. Who had cast a "spell" over them? Paul asks. "Before their eyes Jesus Christ had been evidently set forth, crucified among them."

"Openly set forth" (RV) is the translation of a verb that means "to write beforehand", but which also has the meaning of publicity, by publishing on notice boards or by depicting, or placarding. Taking the literal meaning of the word some have thought the reference was to an earlier letter of Paul to them. But if we have caught aright the tone of the last few verses of chapter 2, and recognized that Paul is there recalling what he had said when he preached Christ unto them, it is evident that the idea of placarding suits the context best. Vividly indeed had Paul set before them the crucified Messiah—how vividly we ourselves can recognise to-day as we read Paul's words. He had made them see Christ; he had made them realise how acceptance of Christ was only possible by identifying themselves with him in that act of crucifying the flesh. He had set before them with an earnestness that was a mark of truth his own experience as a persecutor and then as a follower, and also how the grace and mercy of God in forgiveness of sins was centred in Christ and available for all. Jesus had been "crucified among them" as Paul had recounted it all—even as if they had been present and witnessed the actual transactions outside the city of Jerusalem.

## Divine Approval

Paul passes from his own portrayal of Christ crucified to their experience after his message had been received by them. That experience was an unmistakable proof of divine approval, and was a witness to the truth of the apostle's message in the first generation of disciples.

Turning to the Acts of the Apostles, we find the promise that the apostles would receive divine power "after that the Holy Spirit had come upon them" (1:8). At Pentecost the promise was fulfilled when with a sound of a rushing mighty wind and the appearance of cloven tongues as of fire, the apostles "were all filled with the Holy Spirit" with the immediate effect of enabling them to speak "with other tongues as the Spirit gave them utterance" (2:4). The same power enabled Peter and John to heal a man in the Temple porch, with a consequent testimony concerning God's work in Christ Jesus (3:1–26). This power was manifest in many ways: in the detection of the deception of Ananias and Sapphira (5:1–11); in healing many (5:15,16); in the powerful testimony of Stephen (6:8). From the incident of Philip in Samaria it would appear that the possession of the Spirit did not confer the power to pass the gift to others. Philip could heal (8:7); but the apostles visiting Samaria to see the work Philip was doing, prayed for the new converts that they might receive the Holy Spirit. The apostles then laid their hands upon them and the gift was bestowed (8:15–17).

The case of Cornelius is interesting in this connection. He was instructed in a dream to send for Peter; the apostle at the same time by dream being informed of the visit of the servants of Cornelius. Peter visited Cornelius, preached the gospel, and "the Holy Spirit fell upon all that heard the word" (10:44). Such a mark of God's approval did not permit of any doubt whether the Gentile Cornelius should be baptized, and so the official opening of the Way to Gentiles opened up the larger field of work for which Paul had been prepared in the years intervening from his conversion.

The establishment of the Pauline churches was accompanied with and confirmed by the outpouring of the Spirit. Thus at Iconium "the disciples were filled with joy, and with the Holy Spirit" (13:52). Paul organized the ecclesias where the truth was received, "ordaining elders in every church" (14:23).

It is reasonable to conclude that with the appointment of elders the gifts of the Spirit would be bestowed. The elders among them had the various gifts enumerated by Paul in 1 Corinthians 12 and 14—we may read those chapters as an indication of the endowment of a first century ecclesia, by which, in the absence of the New Testament, they were equipped for the work of the ministry in its various aspects (see the exposition of *The Letter to the Ephesians* on 4:11–13 for the significance of an important passage in this connection). There was thus a permanent witness in each ecclesia of the divine will, and evidence of the fact that God was working with them.

### The Galatians' Experience

With this background we can follow Paul's thought as he appeals to the experience of the Galatians at the time and since he brought the gospel to them.

Paul's message was delivered "in demonstration of the spirit and of power" (1 Corinthians 2:4), and the "testimony was confirmed" in the Corinthians "so that ye come behind in no gift" (1 Corinthians 1:6,7), being "enriched by him in all utterance and all knowledge". What happened in Corinth would not be different from the experience of other ecclesias, and the Galatians would, therefore, see the evidence of divine witness in Paul and would experience among themselves in the spirit gifts bestowed a personal evidence of God working with them.

Paul asks them upon what basis these gifts were bestowed. Did the gifts follow his preaching of the gospel, or the efforts of the Judaizers to win them to observance of law? "This only would I learn of you, Received ye the Spirit by the works of the law, or by the hearing of faith?" Faith, not works of law, was the approved condition of divine favour. By "hearing" not "working", by "faith" and not by "law", did they make themselves approved of God. "Are ye so foolish?" continues Paul, "Having begun in the Spirit, are ye now made perfect by the flesh?" (3:3).

Their initiation was evidently right—the Spirit gifts being witness—but in turning to law they were turning to a method which had no accompanying evidence of God's approval; they were in fact seeking to go on to perfection by a method which had marks of failure. For the contrasted "Spirit" and "flesh" stand here for the grace and blessing of life by the gospel, and the way of fleshly ordinances. The words describe the two sources of their life. The spirit-word of God had begotten in them a new life, by which they worshipped God in spirit and in truth (John 4:23), serving him not in oldness of letter but in newness of spirit: this new life was "Christ in them" or, as the same thought is expressed in the context of that phrase, "the spirit of Christ" and "the Spirit of God" in them (Romans 8:9,10). The flesh was the domain of the old self with its delight in outward ordinances and its pride in self-achievement. Therefore it was inevitable that law was weak through the flesh to condemn sin in the flesh, as Paul affirms in Romans 8:1–4; and it was necessary God should send His own Son in the likeness of sinful flesh, that sin might be there condemned, and an offering for sin in that way provided. To seek perfection by the flesh was to follow man's way of merit; but to encourage the new life by the nourishment of faith was the way of God, by man's trust in God to the glory of God's grace. The absurdity of their action was evident by the mere statement of the case.

In a parenthetic aside Paul makes an appeal to other experiences—this time to the sufferings. They had suffered many things for their adherence to the gospel. Luke tells of Jewish opposition to them, and of joint assault of Jew and Gentile. Paul had told them that it was by much tribulation they must enter into the Kingdom of God (Acts 14:2,5,22). Faith in the gospel led to tribulation; tribulation was a discipline, in turn working patience, experience and hope (Romans 5:3,4), and was therefore part of God's training (Hebrews 12:6). These things belonged to the way of faith; if they followed the way of law there would be no Jewish persecution, and their past sufferings were therefore needless: they had been endured in vain. But Paul will not yet allow that to be the end; he is hopeful of their recovery, and adds: "if it be yet in vain".

Paul draws his conclusion by first restating his question and then by a Scripture quotation: "He (God) therefore that ministereth to you the Spirit, and worketh miracles among you, doeth he it by the works of the law, or by the hearing of faith?" God had worked miracles through Paul, and Paul's message to which they responded and upon which response they had received spirit gifts themselves, was a proclamation of God's grace, which they had heard and in which they had put faith. "Works of law" was the "gospel" of Paul's enemies, who were also enemies of the cross of Christ.

The Scripture quotation is the vital statement of Genesis 15:6. Abraham believed God and it was accounted to him for righteousness. This divine record in Genesis stands written for all generations as the illustration of the divine rule of blessing. Faith in what God has promised is the basis of God's forgiveness of sin by which a man is reckoned righteous in God's sight. The cardinal importance of the passage is seen in the reasoned argument of Romans 4 at the close of which Paul declares the record in Genesis 15:6 was not written for Abraham alone but *for us*, if we believe. God is One, and the condition of favour is one, whether the recipient be Abraham, a descendant of Abraham or a Gentile. The mere statement of the divinely recorded fact that God so reacted to Abraham's faith settles the question. The reference to Abraham, to his faith and his justification, however, not only decides the issue between "faith" and "works", but provides the basis upon which Paul draws out the implications of the divine promises of blessing which God made to Abraham.

### FAITH THE CONDITION OF BLESSING (3:7–9)

IN verse 6 Paul had turned to the Scripture to answer the question whether in their experience works of law or faith was the condition of divine favour. The evidence of experience showed that God's spirit-gifts had followed faith and not works of law; that the gospel of grace preached by Paul, and not the law of works preached by the circumcisers, had received the divine blessing. But experience, even of spirit-gifts, was not in itself sufficient proof. In the first letter to the Corinthians Paul refers to the experience of ecstasies in the pagan worship, and demands that all such phenomena be brought to the test of revealed truth (1 Corinthians 12:1–3). In this letter Paul finds in Scripture the evidence that justi-fication was by faith, and this authoritative endorsement is added to the evidence of its truth which the Galatians had in the possession of the spirit-gifts. The verse quoted (Genesis 15:6) was a classic; it was discussed in the Jewish schools and was familiar to all who knew the Old Testament. Abraham's case, by common consent, was a test; he was the head of the nation, and had been called the friend of God. The choice of the nation was due to the privileged standing of Abraham before God. Three times does Paul in his writings cite Genesis 15:6; twice in Romans (4:3,22); and here in Galatians. The passage is conclusive in Paul's favour: Abraham *believed* God—it was *faith* that was counted to him for righteousness.

The testimony (Genesis 15:6) concerning God's response to Abraham's faith could not be a statement having reference only to Abraham. God deals with men on principles universal in application. Paul the earnest believer in the unity of God saw that if there was only ONE God, then He must be the God of both Jew and Gentile, and further, He must have one rule of justification since all men shared a common need (see Romans 3:26–31, RV). But the One-ness of God involved other things as well: there is one rule of acceptability, and one result of grace—the same blessing upon all where the conditions are observed. The thought of divine unity goes further: in the ultimate issue of the divine redemption all must be one with God, all sharing a divine unity. This higher thought comes out in the later verses of chapter three.

## The True Seed of Abraham

"Ye perceive therefore" (RV margin), says Paul, drawing out the consequence of the divine procedure with Abraham, recorded in Genesis 15:6, "that they which are of faith, the same are the children of Abraham." "We have Abraham to our father", was the proud boast of the Jews—a boast which the Baptist thrust aside with the rejoinder that God could raise up of the stones children to Abraham (Matthew 3:9); mere physical descent conferred no title to Abraham's property, for, were it so, Ishmaelite and Edomite could both prefer a claim. If there were reasons for their rejection—and this no Jew would dispute—there could equally be reasons for the rejection of the descendants of Sarah. Faith was all-important with Abraham; there could be no favour with God when faith was absent. Only faith then on the part of other men established a relationship to Abraham—a fact which excluded many Jews, but which also included many Gentiles.

Paul declares that "they which are of faith" are Abraham's "sons"; "the same are sons of Abraham" (Galatians 3:7, RV)—the absence of the article throwing all the emphasis on the status of sons. But if sonship is based on faith, and is independent of physical relationship, it follows (1) that Abraham's family in God's final purpose must be spiritual and not racial, and (2) since so many are "of faith" who are not of Abraham's descendants, "sonship" in their case must be by adoption.

Heirship follows from sonship. "If children, then heirs" (Romans 8:17), states the two as condition and consequence. Their inevitable connection in Paul's mind would lead us to expect the fact to have a place in his argument. So it has. "Abraham's seed and heirs" (Galatians 3:29) brings together in one phrase the two things. The implied idea of "adoption" in the fact of sonship of those not natural sons, and the further thought of heirship that springs from sonship, comes later in the chapter. But Paul must first show that Abraham's family has for its basis of union faith and not flesh. He does this by turning again to God's words to Abraham recorded in Scripture, "And the scripture, foreseeing that God would jus-

50

tify the heathen (the Gentiles) through faith, preached before the gospel unto Abraham, saying, In thee shall all nations be blessed" (3:8).

The style of this appeal to Scripture is instructive. The apostle and his readers all regarded the Scriptures as the authoritative revelation of God. The argument is based upon *the words* of Scripture; in a later verse upon *one word*. By a figure Paul attributes to the writings the quality of foreknowledge which belongs to God, which could only be done if these writings were of divine authorship. Foreknowledge is of the very essence of the gospel: for the gospel concerns the future, being "glad tidings" of the divine purpose to be accomplished. The modern attitude which disparages foretelling as a function of the prophet, would deprive the gospel of all content. Salvation is based upon God's promise which concerns a future, and is therefore of the nature of prophecy.

"In thee shall all nations be blessed" was God's promise to Abraham before he left his native Ur to go to the land of promise (Genesis 12:3). This purpose was repeated as the ground of God's communication concerning the overthrow of Sodom. "Shall I hide from Abraham that thing which I do; seeing that Abraham shall surely become a great and mighty nation, and all the nations of the earth shall be blessed in him?" (Genesis 18:17,18). What is the blessing here promised? We perhaps think firstly of the material blessings of Christ's reign, the era of peace, the establishment of justice, the abundance of food; houses for all; security based on law; the removal of tyranny, bloodshed, oppression and torture of all forms; the bringing of enlightenment, and love of the things that are best, to all. It is true that these things are included, as the glowing pictures of the prophets of the coming age abundantly show: but they are not the first or the most important blessing. Paul quotes the words: "In thee shall *all the nations* be blessed" as proof that God would justify the Gentiles through faith. "All the nations" included Gentiles as well as Jews—clearly, therefore, the blessing of Abraham is for Gentiles. The proof that God would *justify* them lies in the word "blessed"—in other words, when God said the nations would be blessed the promise concerned the justification of the nations.

**Justification**

What is justification? The answer is well given in the pamphlet *The Atonement*:

51

"This word has two senses which should be clearly distinguished: 1: vindication, declaring to be just; and 2: absolution, acquittal, forgiveness, reconciliation.

"In the first sense our Lord alone is *justified*. The spirit of Christ in Isaiah said: 'The Lord God will help me; therefore shall I not be confounded; therefore have I set my face like a flint, and I know that I shall not be ashamed. He is near that *justifieth* me; who will contend with me?' (Isaiah 50:7,8). And Jesus himself afterwards put it to the Jews: 'Which of *you* convicteth ME of sin?' (John 8:46). And though they adjudged him 'a sinner' (John 9:24), and with the Romans put him to death as such, God raised him from the dead to eternal life and thus 'justified' him in the sense of *vindicated* him; openly declaring him before all men to be 'the only begotten Son of God' in whom the Father was well pleased (Romans 1:4).

"In the second sense of '*justification*' the *adopted* sons and daughters of God are all absolved, acquitted, forgiven, reconciled to God by His grace through faith and repentance, and (after the sacrifice of Christ) by baptism into the name of Jesus Christ, and by 'good works which God hath before ordained that we should walk in them' (Ephesians 2:10). The spirit of Christ in Isaiah had likewise spoken of this saying, 'By his knowledge shall my righteous servant *justify* many; for he shall *bear their iniquities*' (Isaiah 53:11)."

To be justified by God is to be pronounced righteous by Him, and for every son of Adam with the exception of the Lord Jesus, this involves the forgiveness of sins. The parallel in Isaiah 53:11 establishes this: "By his knowledge shall my righteous servant *justify* many; for he shall *bear their iniquities*."

A similar parallel is found in Paul's writings: the death and resurrection of Jesus are connected facts, "delivered for our offences" and "raised for our justification" are equally connected; Christ died for our offences that we may have the forgiveness of sins, or be justified. "For us also, to whom it (righteousness) shall be imputed, if we believe on him that raised up Jesus our Lord from the dead; who was delivered for our offences, and was raised again for our justification" (Romans 4:24,25). The condition on our part—faith—is expressed in the phrase "if we believe", and again in the next verse by the noun "faith". "Therefore being justified by faith, we have peace with God through our Lord Jesus Christ" (5:1). A further synonym with justification is found in the words of

Genesis 15:6, "it (faith) was *counted* to him *for righteous-ness*", a statement which is the subject of discussion through-out the fourth chapter of Romans at the end of which Paul says, as quoted above, that the statement in Genesis was not written for Abraham's sake alone but for us also who believe.

This important significance of the word "blessing" as equal to justification is not limited in its use to the promises to Abraham. "To him that worketh not, but *believeth* on him that justifieth the ungodly, his faith is counted for righteous-ness. Even as David also describeth the *blessedness* of the man unto whom God imputeth righteousness without works, saying, *Blessed* are they whose sins are covered. Blessed is the man to whom the Lord will not impute sin" (Romans 4:5-8).

"Blessed" used by David is a verbal link with the Abrahamic promises of "blessing", and in Paul's interpreta-tion the meaning to be attached to the word in those promis-es is to be found in David's very fervent personal statement about iniquities forgiven and sins covered.

### The Promises of Blessing

We might easily think that such an interpretation belongs only to the closely reasoned doctrinal statements of Paul, but so thinking we should betray our own failure to grasp the messages of the other apostles. Peter preceded Paul in draw-ing out the implication of the promises of blessing. To the Jews of Jerusalem, gathered in one of the Temple courts, Peter concluded an address on God's work in Christ with the words:

> "Ye are the children of the prophets, and of the covenant which God made with our fathers, saying unto Abraham, And in thy seed shall all the kindreds of the earth be blessed. Unto you first God, having raised up his Son Jesus, sent him to bless you, in turning away every one of you from his iniquities." (Acts 3:25,26)

All the kindreds of the earth are to be blessed, but God was sending to the Jews first, with the proffered blessing in the one whom God had raised up first in the line of Abraham, and then raised from death, "turning away every one of you from his iniquities".

Examining this phrase of Peter's—"turning from iniqui-ties"—we observe first of all the difference in form between it and Paul's term "justification" which Paul equates with ini-quities forgiven and sin covered. Is there a difference in point of view? We notice next that Peter is quoting Isaiah. In Acts

3:13,26; 4:27,30 the RV translates "servant" in place of "son" in the AV. This is doubtless correct—the usage being similar to calling a native servant "boy". But this change in the RV at once takes us to Isaiah's prophecies, particularly chapter 53. To the parallel phrases of Isaiah 53:11, already quoted, we may add those of verse 12: "He hath poured out his soul unto death, and he was numbered with the transgressors: yet he *bare the sin of many*, and *made intercession* for the transgressors".

Peter had called upon them to "Repent and *turn again that your sins may be blotted out*" (Acts 3:19). To turn from iniquities is to have done with them, first as something forgiven, and then as repudiating them as the course of life. In particular for Peter's hearers it meant no longer regarding Jesus as an impostor whose crucifixion was a just desert for a blasphemer, but to recognise him as God's servant through whose pouring out of his soul and resurrection he was established as their Messiah. It meant a change of mind and of heart, confessing that, though done in ignorance, they yet had killed the Prince of life. With confession on their part, and the intercession of the Servant, though transgressors their iniquities would be put away by God. Peter's thought is shaped by the prophetic language of Isaiah, but Peter puts the emphasis on the effect upon his hearers of God's work in Jesus.

A third point of contact with Isaiah 53 should be noticed. Peter had healed a lame man, who had entered into the temple "walking and leaping, and praising God". Peter disclaimed any personal power to perform such a miracle. The man had been "made strong" and "given perfect soundness" through faith in the name of Jesus. Jesus, whom they had crucified, lived, and was powerful to heal. So Isaiah had foretold: "By his stripes we are healed" (53:5); and while Peter apparently in his address leaves that application to be drawn by his hearers themselves, or is prevented from making it himself by the interruption which closed the address (Acts 4:1), in his first epistle he speaks of Christ in "his own self bearing our sins in his body on the tree, that we having died to sins might live unto righteousness; by whose stripes we are healed". "Turning from iniquities", then, is to recognise them as borne away, as something to which one has died. Peter completes the thought: "Ye were as sheep going astray, but are now *returned* unto the Shepherd and Bishop of your souls" (1 Peter 2:24,25). To "turn from iniquities" is "turning" to God.

Thus both Peter and Paul explain the covenant blessing with Abraham as forgiveness of sin and fellowship with God, and Peter would say with Paul, "So then, they which be of faith are blessed with faithful (believing—full of faith) Abraham" (Galatians 3:9).

## WORKS OF LAW BRING CURSE (3:10–12)

IF faith, as Paul has shown, is the condition of blessing, of what service was the Law? God had given Israel the Law— what purpose did it serve? What was the result of the efforts of men to keep it, and what was the relation of the Law to life? These and other questions would naturally arise in the minds of those who were advocates of keeping the Law and of those who through their influence were in doubt whether the Law should be observed by them. These questions are dealt with by the Apostle as his argument develops.

Nations are to be blessed, Paul has established, upon the condition of faith; and he now shows that so far from the Law being a means of blessing, the nation that was under the Law and boasted in it found themselves thereby under a curse. This was a turning of the tables upon the Judaisers. They were despising the means of blessing and advocating the course that brought cursing.

Paul puts it boldly: "For as many as are of the works of the law are under the curse: for it is written, Cursed is every one that continueth not in all things which are written in the book of the law to do them" (verse 10). The RV margin "works of law" makes the apostle's statement cover any law: the Mosaic was, of course, the one in view, but what was true of the Mosaic was true of any law, and therefore Paul states his case in the broadest terms. If he establishes the principles then any law is covered: besides which it is essential that he should get at the basic objection to law as a condition of divine favour and the bestowal of life.

When men seek salvation by works they are moved by a desire for self-achievement, seeking to be independent of God. In this respect self-justification resembles Adam's sin, which, springing from a desire to be as God, exalted Adam's own will and disregarded the will of God. Self-righteousness, exalting self, perpetuates the sin of Adam. Fallen man should humbly accept God's grace; but instead of walking in humility, in seeking righteousness by his own efforts he manifests arrogance and pride. His efforts begin and end with pride;

55

blinded by self-esteem a man becomes increasingly satisfied with his own efforts, and less aware of his folly.

The fundamental issue between Jesus and the Pharisees may be found here. "He willing to justify himself" defines the very basis of human effort. "I fast, I tithe"—I do—the odious effects upon a man of his self-centering labour is sketched by Jesus in the parable of the Pharisee and the Publican. Works are like the lush growth of a tree that bears no fruit. "Make the tree good" is the divine rule.

The law of works isolates a man. He inevitably compares himself with others and seeks to excel. But works are things outwardly expressed and are therefore external: and the whole judgement is fixed on act and not motive—it is a judgement by appearances. Thus such a man regards himself as apart from his fellows; his achievements distinguish him from them.

In contrast, the divine way brings home to all men their unworthiness. The best of human labour is seen to have some taint of sin. Whenever God has chosen men for some great duty and has prepared them for it by the vision of His holiness, their complete unfitness for divine use has been realised: "I am a man of unclean lips", said Isaiah, when he had heard the threefold acclamation of God's holiness. This was not because he was base or depraved; on the contrary he was a "holy man of God", chosen to be the channel of the most outstanding revelations of the Messiah. And not only did he realise his own uncleanness of lip, but he felt also that his race, his people, were likewise unclean: "And I dwell in the midst of an unclean people." The sin-conscious man is aware of his oneness with his fellows as members of a sin-enthralled race. Nowhere is the solidarity of the race more clearly seen than in the universality of sinfulness. What the prophet felt in the presence of God was experienced by Peter when he saw that divine power rested on Jesus: "Depart from me, for I am a sinful man, O Lord." The consciousness of unworthiness follows from the conviction of divine truth, but men who hold to the rags of pride and of self-righteousness resist obedience to the truth which involves surrender to God's will. The divine scheme therefore excludes works as the ground of acceptability: in the words of Paul, it is "not of works, lest any man should boast"; or again, "Where is boasting, then? It is excluded: by what law? of works? Nay: but by the law of faith" (Romans 3:27).

In the Galatian letter Paul leaves aside these reasons why salvation is not by law and goes directly to the effect of law.

The law curses: and without exception or variation it curses all under it, for the curse is not graduated according to the extent of disobedience. "To continue in all things written" is the only way to escape the curse. James pointedly states the matter: "Whosoever shall keep the whole law, and yet offend in one point, he is guilty of all" (James 2:10).

The "curse" is written in Deuteronomy 27:26. It involves separation from God, as is evident from the use of the word by Jesus of the rejected: "Depart, ye cursed" (Matthew 25:41). In addition to the negative evidence that the Law did not give salvation since all under it came under its curse, Paul adduces positive evidence that there is another way provided which is radically different from law—the way of faith. "But that no man is justified by the law in the sight of God, it is evident: for, The just shall live by faith" (verse 11). If God has so declared, it is conclusive that God's way of life is not by law.

The verse quoted is found in Habakkuk 2:4 and is used by Paul three times (Romans 1:17; Galatians 3:11; Hebrews 10:38). Its comprehensiveness may be seen by stressing in turn the three elements of the statement. "The just" are those so accounted by God because justified by His grace. They "live" by faith, while the law works death. And faith only is the contribution of the justified—and this faith by its very trust in God excludes self as the ground of sufficiency.

Law and faith are contraries. Strictly the principles are law and grace—works and faith: but Paul gets a greater emphasis by saying that "the law is not of faith". Law does not belong to the same category as faith, for law concerns *doing*, while faith expresses *trusting*.

Difficulty has been found in Paul's citation: "The man that doeth them shall live in them". As it stands, it appears to teach that the law promised life for obedience. It is possible to draw up two lists of passages, one list which appears to support the idea that the law offered life for obedience, and another list categorically the opposite. The Scripture, however, does not contradict itself, and it is obvious that apparent differences must arise from a too restricted view of one set of passages. (See exposition of *Paul's Letter to the Romans*, on chapter 10).

CHRIST AND THE CURSE OF THE LAW (3:13–14)

BECAUSE none kept it perfectly, the Law cursed all under it. So far from its being, as many Jews thought, a means where-

57

by men could attain to life, it was found to be an effective barrier to life—to be in fact something that by its cursing cut men off from life. The Law thus made evident man's impotence and therefore the need for divine action if men were to be saved. Paul has already referred to that divine action in God's Son "who gave himself for our sins" (1:4), "who gave himself for me" in being crucified (2:20). For Paul's argument to be complete, concerning the inefficacy of the Law as a way of life he must not only show that Christ's work met the personal needs of men who are by conduct sinners and by nature death-stricken, but he must also show that Christ has removed the curse of law—the law which not only could not give life, but which sentenced men to death. In fact, if Christ is the Redeemer he must of necessity redeem those under the curse of Law from that curse. The very contrast "Law cursed—Christ redeemed from the curse" is an absolute and final refutation of the Judaisers' claims.

It is Christ who has done this: of course Christ is Jesus—but by saying Christ did it, Paul indicates that it is the Messiah who has removed the curse. He will say in the next breath the curse was removed by his crucifixion—by that very death which was so scandalous in the eyes of the Jew. And instead of the cross demonstrating, as the Jew thought, that the claims of Jesus to be the Messiah were blasphemy, the cross proved that Jesus was the Messiah. Paul here defends his teaching by a frontal attack on the Jewish position, affirming that it was required of the exalted and glorified King of Israel that he should suffer and die for men's sins as a condition of honour and glory—"I will know nothing" says Paul, "but Messiah Jesus and him a crucified one". This argument that Old Testament prophecy demanded that the Messiah must be one who first gave his life as an offering for sins turned the objection of the Jews into a convincing proof to all willing to weigh the evidence. The apostles were not slow to use it; of the many illustrations, Peter in Acts 2 and Paul in Hebrews 2:9,10, are conspicuous examples: but the thought is implicit here when Paul says Christ—the Messiah—hath redeemed us from the curse of the Law.

**The Curse Removed**

How has the curse of the Law been "bought off"?—for so the word translated *redeemed* in this place literally means. Paul answers: by Messiah "being made a curse for us"; for us, not instead of us; but for us in that he has come under the curse of the Law that he might take it away for himself and for us; for us, in that we, by faith identifying ourselves with him in

58

his submission to the curse, share with him in the results, in the removal of the curse from us.

It is clear that when Paul says Christ hath redeemed *us* from the curse of the Law, he means those who were under the law, "us" Jews. But *the principle* by which this curse of law has been taken away is identical with that by which the curse of sin and death has been removed. When the principle in the latter case has been understood, the way in which the law-curse was done away is not difficult to perceive. The one was considered in the exposition of 2:20 to which reference might be made. It is ably set forth in the pamphlets *The Blood of Christ* and *The Slain Lamb*. Let us now follow Paul's thought concerning how Christ has removed the curse of the law. Christ has been "made a curse"; he elsewhere says that he was "made under the law" and while there is a close connection between the two statements, there is greater significance in the phrase "made a curse". If we put the statement in the concrete form instead of the abstract—which Paul was led to use because he had just spoken of the curse of the law in connection with others—then it is declared that Jesus was accursed! This truly makes the statement startling, but we have in no wise altered Paul's sense and at once the parallel suggests itself—he was accursed for us and "he was made sin for us" (2 Corinthians 5:21). Besides being grammatically impossible, we must reject as futile in the light of this parallel the suggestion that by "sin" Paul in this place means "sin-offering". No—Paul means sin, but we must understand what is intended by the word. Christ was made sin in partaking of the nature in which sin reigns and which produces sin, and which therefore by metonymy is called sin. We may go further and say he was made "sin" in enduring the consequences of sin—sin not his own, for he did not sin—but sin which has left its effects upon the whole race of mankind in bringing all under subjection to death. If we recognise how horrible in God's sight sin is, then we see how the effects of it are brought to a focus as it were in His own obedient Son. "Him who knew no sin God made to be sin for us, that we might become the righteousness of God in him."

He was *made to be*—we *become*; the difference being that he felt and endured in his own person the consequences of sin, accepting voluntarily those consequences, whereas we are forgiven our sins and so become the righteousness of God.

He was made "sin" without being a sinner; he was also "made a curse" without transgressing the law. How this came about Paul explains. He was cursed in the mode of death, and

59

this involved no personal responsibility on his part. An edict of the law declared: "Cursed is everyone that hangeth on a tree." Christ was nailed to the tree and so came under the curse.

## "The Tree"

Let us observe that it is not only in this place that emphasis is put on "the tree" in connection with Christ. All the Lord's own references to his impending crucifixion take on an added meaning in the light of it. But the idea recurs in apostolic thought. Thus Peter told the Jewish authorities that God "raised up Jesus, whom ye slew and hanged on a tree" (Acts 5:30); he used the same phrase to Cornelius (10:39). To the Jews of Pisidian Antioch Paul declared that when "they had fulfilled all that was written of him, they took him down from the tree, and laid him in a sepulchre" (13:29). In a very important passage in his first epistle Peter says that Jesus "his own self bare our sins in his own body to the tree". From these statements it is evident that the mode of Christ's death entered conspicuously into the thought of the first Christian teachers when they were explaining the truth to Jews or those with Jewish contacts.

We turn then to consider the passage in the Law which Paul quotes. It appears parenthetically in a commandment that if a man had committed a sin worthy of death, and he be put to death and hung on a tree, then his body must not remain on the tree beyond nightfall, that the land be not defiled. The reason given is that "he that is hanged is accursed of God". Some effort has been made to confine the curse of the Law to the penal death imposed for sin, on the ground that it seems needless to add a curse for the mere exposure of the body—a view that would limit the curse to the man who had died because of transgression. But the statement which explains why the body exposed on the tree must be removed is general and not confined to the criminal. When the criminal is hung on a tree there is added to the sentence which brings him to death the curse which his exposure brings. A man innocent of transgression of which he was accused and for which he was sentenced to death would by the hanging come under the curse. This is not hypothetical, for it is what actually happened in the case of the Lord, Paul himself being witness. Christ became a curse because he hung upon a tree.

The explanation may be found in the fact that the Law dealt with actual transgression and also with defilement that might even come upon a person innocently. This ceremonial defilement could come in many ways, but the most striking are those that came by obeying the Law itself. Thus Aaron had to wash after the offering in the Holiest of All on the Day of Atonement. The man who bore the ashes of the offering without the camp on the same day had also to wash (Leviticus 16). The priest who had charge of the burning of the red heifer, the ashes of which were to be added to the waters of separation for the cleansing of defilement contracted by touching anything dead, had to wash and was unclean until the evening. The man who removed the ashes was unclean until the even. Even the ministers of the rite of cleansing for this defilement were considered to be unclean (Numbers 19). Thus the very operations enjoined by God for cleansing produced a ceremonial defilement. The law was rigorous, for the man who neglected the purification rites when he contracted defilement had to be cut off. A man could thus be defiled by the law even in fulfilling it.

The pollution occasioned by these enactments of the law were altogether independent of moral guiltiness. But the Law does not discriminate in its operation between moral and ceremonial guilt. We cannot separate the moral code from the ceremonial in the Law of Moses: the Law is one—so much so, that a man who offended in one particular was guilty of all.

Jesus then, Paul tells us, in the mode of his death, came under the Law's curse. In this transaction he was himself innocent, and in his case the time when the curse came upon him coincided with the accepting of the full penalty of the curse of the Law. Death was the penalty the Law imposed. Jesus was cursed in the form in which death came and the full claims of the Law were met by his death, while his sinless life ensured his resurrection. The Law could make no further claims upon him, and he passed from under its operation when he died, and thus by his death the Law which cursed him was done away.

## "Dead to the Law"

All persons under the Law were cursed. How could the curse on them be removed? The answer is, by identification with Jesus and sharing his death, and so sharing the fruits of his victory. Only thus could the curse of the Law be removed; and all who are crucified with Christ become in Paul's phrase, "dead to the law".

The Law could not remove sin; it convicted of sin. Men under the Law must have a redeemer. The redemption came by Christ's death; in Paul's words, he "is the mediator of the new testament, that by means of death, for *the redemption of the transgressions that were under the first covenant,* they which are called might receive the promise of eternal inheritance". Some very helpful comments related to this subject are to be found in *The Law of Moses,* chapters 18 and 28.

When we perceive Paul's reasoning based upon the clause about hanging on a tree, it would seem reasonable to conclude that its insertion in the Law was a divine provision for the working out of God's purpose. Under the Roman rule he met his death by crucifixion; earlier or later in time, and death would not normally have been so inflicted. The "fulness of time" brought together the man and the circumstances which fulfilled God's purpose.

The effect of Christ being made a curse for us (verse 13) is twofold—each effect being introduced by "that": "That the blessing of Abraham might come on the Gentiles through Jesus Christ; that we might receive the promise of the Spirit through faith" (verse 14).

In the two phrases "blessing of Abraham" and "promise of the Spirit" we have illustrations of the ambiguity that can attach to the use of the genitive—that is, a phrase beginning with the preposition "of". Is the first the blessings that Abraham can bestow; the blessing that belongs to Abraham which might be shared; or the blessing referred to in the promises made to him to be bestowed upon all nations? Is "the promise of the Spirit", a reference back to verse 2; or the Spirit in the sense of the new man in Christ begotten by the word as used in Romans 8; or the Spirit promised in the change of physical nature at the resurrection; or is it the promise made by the Spirit in Paul, the agent used by the Spirit; or is the word used by metonymy for God, who uses the Spirit to accomplish His purposes?

The answer is found by keeping in mind the immediate context and also the broad teaching of the Scripture. In verse 8 Paul explained that justification, the forgiveness of sins, was the essence of the blessing promised to Abraham and his seed: hence he concluded (verse 9) that they "which be of faith are blessed with faithful Abraham". The blessing is reconciliation with God through His forbearance in passing by sins and so introducing to His favour. This is the blessing God indicated to Abraham that should come to all nations.

For what reason, then, does Paul say that this blessing can now come on the Gentiles as a consequence of Christ having borne the curse of the Law? The answer is that so long as the Law was in operation it was not possible for Gentiles to come to God except through association with the nation of Israel and so through the Law. The Jewish nation was the channel of favour—and God's arrangements for worship were embodied in the Law given to Israel. To observe the Law a stranger must become associated with the nation of God. But when Christ took the curse of the Law upon him and so put the Law away, a new arrangement became operative. The Lord himself announced this change to the woman of Samaria:

"But the hour cometh, and now is, when the true worshippers shall worship the Father in spirit and in truth: for the Father seeketh such to worship him. God is a Spirit: and they that worship him must worship him in spirit and in truth." (John 4:23,24)

After his resurrection, therefore, Jesus commanded that the proclamation of the gospel should be made to all nations. The new covenant (the Abrahamic) had been ratified by Christ's own blood (Matthew 26:28), and thenceforward the apostles, as "ministers of the new covenant" (2 Corinthians 3:6) invited all men to become heirs of the Abrahamic promises.

The second effect—"that we might receive the promise of the Spirit through faith"—is easily understood when it is recognised that the operative word is "promise". God had made promises to Abraham. Paul immediately refers specifically to them in verse 16: "Now to Abraham and his seed were the promises made", and in verse 29 "Ye (in Christ) are heirs according to the promise". These two references make it practically certain that when Paul uses the word "promise" in verse 14, he means the promise that was made to Abraham. Why is it then called "the promise of the Spirit"? Because the Spirit was the agent employed by God in making it known, and by Spirit is meant God (the agent by a figure being put for the principal). Read it as "the promise of God" and the sense is clear. But figures of speech are not used arbitrarily: by their introduction something is added. When God is called the "Fear of Isaac" it denotes that He was the God of Isaac and also One whom Isaac reverenced. Paul had been arguing in verse 2 that through the gospel they had received the gifts of the Spirit as confirmation of its truth. By speaking of the promise of the Spirit, Paul indicates that the same God who had wrought in their midst such confirmation of Paul's gospel, was the One who by His Spirit had revealed His will and purpose in the past and now confirmed the inclusion of the Gentiles by the guidance of the same Spirit in the apostles. We would emphasise that Paul is not thinking of the bestowal of spirit-gifts as something promised. His thought

63

goes much deeper than that. The promise was received "through faith", for faith was the condition upon which Abraham was accepted, and men only became heirs of the promise by faith.

The conclusion drawn in verse 14 bore in a practical way upon the position of the Galatians. Their Jewish seducers were taking them back to the method in operation before Christ's death, and in such a way as would bring them under the curse of law. But Christ's death resulted in the invitation to share in God's salvation being taken to Gentiles: the Galatians were going back in time and back in advantage; they were, therefore, missing present blessings and favours which were now available apart from the unbearable burden of the Law. They might go back, but not so Paul. Nor would they go back at all if he could take them forward. How persuasively he does this when he uses the pronoun "we"! He joins himself with them as one to whom the promise has come by faith: it is not "you" but "we"—I, Paul, the bearer of the glad tidings, and you, my converts, who received the good news.

### PROMISE NOT DISANNULLED BY LAW (3:15–18)

HISTORY (see Galatians 3:6; Genesis 15:6) and promise (Galatians 3:8; Genesis 12:3) both testified that it was by faith a man was justified; moreover Law brought upon man a curse (Galatians 3:10; Deuteronomy 27:26). Understandably, the Jewish Christians felt the question why God gave the Law at all to be a practical one, and one that called for answer. To this question therefore, Paul now turns, first showing that the Law given after the promise did not invalidate the promise.

He begins his argument by an acknowledged human illustration: "Brethren, I speak after the manner of men; though it be but a man's covenant, yet if it be confirmed, no man disannulleth, or addeth thereto" (verse 15).

Much ink has been spilt about the meaning of the word "covenant". The Greek word for covenant common in classical Greek and in papyri and inscriptions, is *suntheke*. But Paul uses the word *diatheke*, which normally means testament, disposition, will. The translation of the word by *testament* has influenced the names by which today we distinguish the two portions of the Scriptures. On the other hand, the Septuagint translation of the Old Testament uses *diatheke* to translate the Hebrew word *berith*, which, without question, means covenant. This use is practically uniform, only about five exceptions being noted in Hatch & Redpath's *Concordance to the LXX*. This practice of the LXX to use *diathēkē* for covenant is sufficient to fix its usage among Greek-speaking readers of the Old Testament. But the matter is capable of a practical test. Jeremiah 31:31 speaks of a new covenant God will make with Israel. The old covenant was made at Sinai and was confirmed with the sprinkled blood of animals. The new covenant in contrast to the old covenant provides for the forgiveness of sins, and this requires that it be confirmed with "better sacrifices" than the old covenant (Hebrews 10:16,17; 8:6; 9:23). That the better confirming-sacrifice is the offering of Jesus, is placed beyond all doubt by his own words: "This is my blood of the new covenant shed for many for the remission of sins" (Matthew 26:28). The word *diathēkē* is thus used in the New Testament as equivalent to the Old Testament "covenant" and the Old Testament meaning is the one that must be attached to the word in the New Testament. In fact the idea of covenant is involved in all the New Testament occurrences of the word.

A good suggestion why the LXX used *diathēkē* for *berith* is that since the Greek custom of testamentary disposition indicated by the word was unknown among the Hebrews, the word was adopted and applied to the covenant between God and His people. "As this was the outcome of God's sovereign grace and bounty, and not a matter of mutual arrangement" (says F. G. Rendall), "it could hardly be described by any of the Greek terms for covenant; it was on the other hand analogous to a disposition of property by testament and was accordingly designated by the term *diathēkē*." God's gifts to Abraham are "covenants of promise", and of these Paul is speaking. The sense of the word is therefore not in doubt, and it is not necessary to pursue the arguments which have been advanced by many scholars, whether Paul is here thinking of Greek or Roman forms of a "will". The Old Testament provides the facts upon which the apostle is basing his argument, and therefore fixes the meaning of the words used.

Paul's argument is general. When a man makes a disposition or covenant and it is confirmed, it is outside the power of anyone else to annul or add thereto. Has God added anything that affects the promise? Paul will show that while the Law came after, it did not affect the provisions of the promise: but first he establishes the facts by which he will prove his doctrine.

65

Verse 16 is very familiar to all who reason out of the Scriptures concerning the purpose of God revealed in the Old Testament. Without in any way detracting from the usual use of the verse, let us see its meaning in its context. As a man's covenant is unalterable by subsequent happenings so with God's covenant with Abraham (and we mark that Paul equates covenant with promise in what he now says): "Now to Abraham and his seed were the promises made. He saith not, And to seeds, as of many; but as of one, And to thy seed, which is Christ."

## The Priority of the Promise

The promise was made to Abraham, and it therefore preceded the Law by some four hundred years. In time, the promise has priority; secondly, God's intentions were expressed in the form of *promises*, and promises are not legal agreements—two-sided—they come spontaneously from a giver to a recipient; thirdly, the promises are to Abraham and his seed—not many seeds, but one seed, as Paul points out.

Previously the apostle has said that they which are of faith are the children of Abraham (verse 7). Kinship with Abraham in these matters is not based upon flesh descent but upon spiritual harmony. The true family of Abraham are all one in thought and purpose. Moreover, they are one with God because by their association with Abraham they are also "children of God" (verse 26).

Paul says that the seed is *one*, and while we first think of this as an arithmetical definition, we find that it contains also the larger conception of a divine unity. The word "one" recurs in verses 20 and 28 and is a link in Paul's argument. The selection of "the seed" is historically illustrated in God's dealings with Abraham's descendants. Of the two sons Isaac and Ishmael (the subject of a profound allegory in chapter 4), Isaac was chosen while Ishmael was cast out. Of Isaac's twin sons Esau was rejected and Jacob chosen. The "purpose of God according to election" is in this shown, and "the children of the promise" are counted for "the seed" (Romans 9:7–13). All these "children" form together "one body" in Christ: they are the body of which Christ is the head, and being "his body", they are, in a very pregnant phrase, "the fulness of him that filleth all in all" (Ephesians 1:22,23).

When Ishmaelites and Edomites were under consideration the Jew readily discounted flesh descent. Paul says the discount is equally to be made with all flesh descent—a profane Jew was no better than an unbelieving Arab. This does not mean that national Israel are cut off from their privilege of

66

being God's firstborn national son; the gifts and calling of God are not subject to change of mind, as Paul says. But inclusion in a national "seed" confers no spiritual advantage, for that depends upon the spiritual qualities of faith and obedience.

The "one seed" is Christ—Messiah—whoever may prove to be Christ. His identity was to Paul and his readers not in dispute, and the changes are rung, not without a reason, on the titles, "faith of Jesus Christ" (verse 22), "faith in Christ Jesus" (verse 26), "baptized into Christ", "put on Christ" (verse 27), "one in Christ Jesus", (verse 28), concluding with: "If ye be Christ's, then are ye Abraham's seed", the "one" seed of the promise.

The steps in Paul's argument 3:15–18 are: (a) A covenant when confirmed cannot be annulled or altered, (b) God had by covenant-promises covenanted certain blessings to Abram, (c) the implications of this in relation to the law. The third item occupies verses 17 and 18 which read:

"And this I say, that the covenant, that was confirmed before of God in Christ, the law, which was four hundred and thirty years after, cannot disannul that it should make the promise of none effect. For if the inheritance be of the law, it is no more of promise: but God gave it to Abraham by promise."

It might first be noticed that the RV on good evidence omits the words "in Christ" in verse 17. It is true that the promises receive their full ratification in Christ, inasmuch as they are not possible of fulfilment apart from his work as the Saviour. Abraham and all past worthies will attain to everlasting life through the offering of the Lord Jesus. But the promises were typically confirmed to Abraham, and that typical confirmation provides the ground for Paul's argument. The covenant with Abraham was confirmed by God before the Law—in point of time the promises preceded the Law by 430 years. The promise came first, and it was confirmed; the Law then cannot annul it, or make it ineffective. The Law cannot be a supplement or modification for law stands in direct antithesis to promise. Law involves works, promise calls for faith; law involves terms of mutual agreement, a promise is spontaneous and free; law ends in condemnation, but God's promise leads to justification. Law and promise then are fundamentally opposed. And further, as a matter of fact, the inheritance is by promise: God gave it by promise: "To thee and thy seed will I *give* this land". And when Abraham asked, "Whereby shall I know that I shall inherit it?" God

67

instructed him to prepare sacrifices; and at close of day a deep sleep, a horror of darkness, representing death, came upon Abraham, and God said, "Know of a surety that thy seed shall be a stranger in a land that is not theirs, and shall serve them; and they shall afflict them four hundred years", but in the fourth generation God would bring them into the land. Then a burning lamp passed between the pieces of the offering by which God, after the practice of so ratifying a covenant, confirmed His covenant with the father of the faithful. The confirmed promise was then re-stated: "Unto thy seed have I *given* this land" (Genesis 15:7–18).

A word might be added upon the time periods. In the quotation given from Genesis, God spoke of 400 years. Paul speaks of an interval of 430 years between the promise and the law. Both statements are correct. While both end with the giving of the Law, the 400 begins with the birth of Isaac—the reference to "thy seed" excluding an earlier commencement. Abraham was then 100 years old. The promise was given 30 years earlier when he would be 70; and since he entered the land of promise when he was 75, the first promise must have been given five years before that entry.

## WHY GOD GAVE ISRAEL THE LAW (3:19–24)

IF the Law did not modify the promise, what was God's purpose in giving it? The answer touches what might be called a Biblical philosophy of history. The Law was operative throughout Israel's national history, and its authority passed with the final overthrow of the nation. That overthrow could be ascribed to many human causes; to Israel's relationship to the rising power of Babylon and later to the spread of the Roman Empire; to the fanatical spirit of Israel; to the inevitable clash of two proud peoples one of whom displayed at that time as great a degree of invincibility as the world has known. But these are the external features; the divine view gives the inner and deeper causes. Before Israel were finally overthrown, but when events were moving towards the catastrophe, the seed of the promise appeared and was rejected. The death of the seed, however, from God's point of view had the effect of annulling the Law. The Law had served its purpose, and the end of that purpose coincided with and was in a real sense connected with the end, for the time being, of the nation as an organised people. Paul says that the Law "was added because of transgressions, till the Seed should come to whom the promise was made" (literally—because of *the* transgressions, i.e., the transgressions of it) (3:19). The

operation of law had the effect of revealing the inward opposition of men to God's will: it brought to the surface the latent
waywardness and wilfulness. The parallels with the Epistle
to the Romans are particularly important as helps in inter-
preting Paul's meaning in this section. "The Law entered that
the offence might abound" (5:20). In chapter 7 he describes
his own experience of law, and from this could testify of its
effects. He was alive without law once as a young Jewish
child. With the knowledge of law, sin, says Paul in a vivid
metaphor, sprang to life, and the living sin wrought death in
Paul (verse 9). He had not known sin, except by the law
(verse 7) and sin, by the commandment became exceedingly
sinful (verse 13). He also affirms that the strength of sin is
the law (1 Corinthians 15:56). The effect of law revealed the
sinfulness of the nature of man, and convinced those under it
that there was a law of sin in their members; law also showed
that sin was opposition to God's will, and that man could not
therefore by law gain for himself, by his own merit, the
favour of God. The operation of law thus brought home to the
conscience of men the holiness of God and the wide gulf
which separated man from God. Israel's pride led them, to a
large extent, to miss for themselves the lesson; but this only
made them the more an object lesson of the unloveliness of
human nature when it depends on its own resources. But
when a man recognises the facts which the working of law
brings to light, he is ready to turn to the proposed mercy of
God revealed in Christ. At the same time, the utter refusal of
Israel to accept the divine overtures in the apostolic messages of God's grace showed the need that God should bring
upon them penalties of the covenant that they had broken.
The Seed thus appeared at a crisis in history.

**The Seed in Prophecy**

The seed is firstly Abraham's seed, but there is a thread of
prophecy which sustains the theme of the Seed. The first
promise concerned the seed of the woman (Genesis 3:15); the
blessing of Judah obliquely refers to it (Genesis 49:10); the
heir to the throne of Israel is the seed of David (2 Samuel
7:12); God was seeking "a godly seed" (Malachi 2:15). In "the
seed" that should come, all these foreshadowings are fulfilled, but, admittedly, the contextual reference in Galatians
is to Abraham's seed.

The Law "was ordained by angels in the hands of a mediator" (3:19). There were, therefore, two links between God,
the Giver of the Law, and His people who received the Law.
Once only did God speak direct, and the people could not bear

it and besought that the experience should not be repeated (Exodus 20:19; Deuteronomy 18:16). God approved their request, but not the motive that prompted it. But out of their desire not to hear again God's voice, came the arrangement that prophets should receive the message from God and then communicate it to the people. At the head of this succession of prophets stood Moses. But there was another intermediary. The "angel of God's presence" (Isaiah 63:9) represented God to Israel. "My name is in him", said God (Exodus 23:20). The angel appeared to Moses at the bush (Exodus 3:2), and the angel "spake to Moses in the Mount Sina", "in the ecclesia in the wilderness" as Stephen reminded his judges, with pointed reference to another "ecclesia" in which the Messiah will render praise (Psalm 22:25). One may wonder whether Stephen's argument was in Paul's thought as he reasons about the Law-mediator and contrasts the higher blessings associated with a seed of promise. In Hebrews 2:2–4 there is a similar contrast between the law and the great salvation; but here the further reference to angels is designed to show the importance of the law, yet only to bring out the much greater importance of the word "spoken by the Lord" Jesus. The law came through God's servants; the gospel is established by and in God's Son.

Moses was the mediator of the covenant, while the angels were the messengers through whom God communicated His will. Moses mediated the old covenant when he announced its terms and received the assent of the people and then "took the blood of calves and of goats, with water, and scarlet wool, and hyssop, and sprinkled both the book, and all the people, saying, This is the blood of the testament which God hath enjoined unto you" (Hebrews 9:19,20).

### The Mediator

The reference to the mediator leads to a comment by Paul which has so perplexed expositors that it is said that 430 explanations have been given. As it stands the statement, "Now a mediator is not a mediator of one", is so obvious a truism—and moreover one which is unmeaning in this context—that it is evident there is a deeper significance attached to the word "one" than simply "one party". It is essential that we keep in mind that in this context by "mediator" Paul is thinking of Moses to whom he has referred by this word in verse 19. What is the "one" of which Moses is not the mediator? So put, the answer at once is evident—the "one" seed of verse 16. Following as it does the reminder of the important media of the giving of the Law—the angels and Moses—the statement nevertheless declares the inadequacy of the work of Moses. The initiation of Israel to God's people is contrasted with the perfect "unity" which is the mark of *one* "seed" promised. Moses and angels mediated the first, but could not establish the second. The divine unity is brought about by more direct divine action. This idea is confirmed by the next phrase, "But God is One", which we must now consider.

It is no mere assertion of monotheism that Paul makes: what relevance would that have in this context? Yet the doctrinal fact that God is One underlies Paul's thought. To the apostle the "one-ness" of God, so definitely declared in the Old Testament (Deuteronomy 6:4), and so fundamental to Jewish thought of God, involved a philosophy of salvation. For while God Himself is One, there is disharmony in His world, both in itself and also in its relation to its Creator. Such disharmony is a challenge to God's nature, and since He is supreme, discord must give place to peace and harmony; as God is one, all that live must become one in Him, acknowledging and rendering the honour and praise that is due to Him. Not only so, but since God is One, He cannot be limited to a "tribal god". If the godhead were many there might be a distribution of the several gods to the various nations, Yahweh being Israel's God. But Yahweh had no peer. "The Lord our God is one Lord." Yahweh Himself asserted that there was no God beside Him. If we turn to the letter to the Romans, we find Paul using this fact of God's "one-ness" to establish the consequent ways in which God deals with men, and this explains the reference in Galatians.

Paul asserts that "a man is justified by faith without the deeds of the law" (Romans 3:28). This rule is universal: for a *man* is any man, whether Jew or Gentile, although the particular channel used for faith's operation may vary. God's method is one for all: otherwise, if there are different methods for Jew and for Gentile God cannot be the same God to all. "Is he the God of the Jews only" Paul asks; meaning that if salvation were by works of law, since God had given only Israel the law, God must then be God only of Israel. "Is he not also of the Gentiles?" Yes, Paul answers, and finds his proof in what was axiomatic to the Jew—God was One: "For if so be that God is One" then He is God of all, Jew and Gentile, and His rule of acceptance must be one for all. God will justify the Jew "out of" faith and the Gentile "through" the Faith. Israel had the revelation of God—"out of faith" in the purpose therein revealed the Jew was justified: to the Gentile the gospel was preached, and the doctrinal items made known for faith in the aggregate constituted "the faith", through which Gentiles were approved. Faith then was the common denominator of both old and new covenant times, the one way of approach for Jew and for Gentile. Faith united men to God and made them one in Him and one with Him.

With this instructive parallel in Romans we can interpret the words of Galatians: "but God is One". Being *one* His purpose must bring men to one-ness with Him. Since the Law emphasised the essential disharmony of human nature with God, Moses the mediator of the Law therefore could not mediate the covenant of the "One"—yet the latter was sure of accomplishment and must then be accomplished by other means. These means Paul has shown to be by the promises, which centre in the One Seed (verse 16), which are operative by faith, by which all become "children of God" and all are "one" in Christ Jesus. The prayer of the Seed whose blood was about to be shed to confirm the covenants of promise, concerned this unity: "I pray ... that they all may be one ... in us" (John 17:20,21).

**God is One**

A further consequence springs from the unity of God. It was recognised that God was the author of both law and promise; but to the Jew there appeared to be an irreconcilable antagonism between the two. This in turn suggested a duality in God, for these two expressions of His mind appeared to conflict. But was there in fact this antagonism? "Is the law against the promises of God?" The opposition was only in the mind of the Jew because of his misunderstanding of the purpose of Law. God being One, there could be no antagonism between His various arrangements. The misunderstood fact was that the Law was never intended as a rival system to the promises. The latter concerned an everlasting inheritance and therefore eternal life to those who received the promise. The Law was not intended to give life—such a method was impossible; had it been possible God would have used it, but because man could not attain to life by Law, God revealed Himself as a Saviour. So Paul adds as a reason for his emphatic repudiation of the suggestion of an opposition between the two: "If there had been a law given which could have given life, verily righteousness should have been by the law" (verse 21). The giving of Law then in no way retracted the gift by promise: on the contrary the Law brought home the impotence of man, and therefore his hopelessness apart from God's grace and gift of life.

With this view Scripture testimony agrees. "The Scripture (for example, the one quoted in verse 10) hath concluded all under sin, that the promise by faith of Jesus Christ might be given to them that believe" (verse 22). This statement is very compressed. God has "shut up" (RV) all. There is a custody enclosing man and his works so completely that he cannot effect an escape. In Romans 11:32, RV, Paul says that "God hath *shut up all* unto disobedience, that he might have mercy upon all": but the statement in Galatians is more comprehensive. The Scripture (that is God, the author) has "shut up *all things* under sin". Sin is a warden; "all things" are under his power, for the best of human efforts, the highest aims, have yet a blemish of sin. "Promise" by metonymy stands for the thing promised—the blessing, which in turn is justification, as we have seen in verse 8. All human efforts being thus marred by sin, only justification by faith in Jesus, who died as a sin offering that sins might be forgiven, can open the way from man's prison house.

The Law was added till the seed should come (verse 19). Until the advent of the Christ, and the consequent preaching of faith in his name, (or, as briefly put in verse 23, "before the faith" came), "we were kept under law" which acted as a guard. It was a guard which was as exacting as sin was powerful, for of both sin and law Paul uses the word "shut up" (verses 22 and 23). This guard, however, had in view a development—"the faith which should afterwards be revealed". The Law then was not an end in itself, but all the time was serving a further aim. It was a shadow of better things to come; its function was like a tutor-slave, or *paedagogus*. His duty, in better households, was to look after the boys of a household who were between seven and seventeen, in a moral, disciplinary and educational service. This was the object of law; it was a servant to guide, instruct and train: but those under its control were juniors who, on reaching majority, passed from the control of the tutor-slave. The fulness of stature of manhood was in Christ: the service of the law lasted in time till Christ came, and its function to instruct concerning him ceased with his coming. Christ having come, the way of justification was historically exhibited by his sacrificial death, his resurrection and the proclamation of forgiveness of sins in his name. The tutor-slave's work was done, for that to which it directed those under his control had come; men might be justified by faith.

SONSHIP IN CHRIST (3:25–29)

"THE FAITH" (verse 23, RV) in the mind of Paul is a system of truth proclaimed for men to believe. It was his mission "to turn men from darkness to light, that they might receive remission of sins and inheritance among them which are sanctified by faith" in Christ. Until Christ's death this "remission of sins in *his name*" was not proclaimed. We have seen that the manifestation of God's Son coincided in time with the end of the law, both in God's purpose and in the consequent historical changes brought about by the dispersion of the Jews. With the teaching of Jesus and that of the apostles we reach the fulness of the revelation of God's purpose. This revelation was gradual; it was not conditioned, however—as modern critical views suggest—by the progress of man's discovery of God's ways, but by the changes in circumstances. The simple promise in Eden was the only way a statement of God's purpose could then be made. The dividing of the human family into nations with the strivings as a consequence for the possession of good and strategically important lands provided the historical conditions for the promise to Abraham of the everlasting possession of the land. The prominence which attached to the throne and the newly established rule by kings in Israel led to the covenant of the throne with David. Everlasting life, everlasting possession of the earth, the rule over the nations with Messiah, are basic elements of the faith. Old Testament revelation included in each of these three "seed" promises the information that the one through whom they would be fulfilled would be the Son of God. When that Son delivered God's message to his generation the fact of his sonship had a prominent place. But not only his own sonship, but the sonship of those who believed in him was set forth. "As many as received him to them gave he power to become sons of God, even to them that believe on his name" (John 1:12). This revelation concerning the status of sons is the essential development in the unfolding of God's purpose of grace to men. "Now are we the sons of God", John wrote. If ye call on God as Father, then, said Peter, be "obedient children" (1 Peter 1:14). "As many as are led by the Spirit of God, they are the sons of God ... ye have received the Spirit of adoption whereby ye cry Abba, Father" (Romans 8:14,15). No higher relation with God than that of sons is possible: with the coming of the Son we have in every sense the fulness of God's revelation, only to be exceeded by what is indeed but the culmination of that relationship, the bestowal of a sonship in immortal nature.

The law, belonging to a dispensation prior to the appearance of God's Son, was a part of the preparatory revelation. Its discipline and the ritual instruction was a tutelage, and there is therefore an aptness in the use by Paul of the figure of the tutor-slave, to which he has compared the Law.

The figure has this further use: with the passing time bringing maturity of his charges, the service of the tutor-slave came to an end. Those under his care have attained the status of sons. This status of sons is essentially of "the faith" now preached; and therefore men are no longer under the tutelage of the Law. By this reasoning Paul leads on the Galatians to see that the development of God's plan has left behind the Law. "But after that the faith is come we are no longer under a schoolmaster." The change from "we" to "ye" in the next verse pointedly recalls to the readers of the epistle that they have left the Law behind: "For ye are are all the children of God by faith in Jesus Christ" (verse 26).

How are they to be regarded as children when they were not really so by birth? Only by adoption. The mode of adoption is by a union with Christ, who was God's Son by begettal. In him they share his sonship. The union with him is effected by a ritual identification with his death and resurrection—by baptism into Christ. That union with Christ is "a putting on of Christ". Paul many times speaks of a "putting on" in which the figure of robing must be given a full significance, but the precise meaning must be determined by the context. In this context Paul is thinking of the passing from childhood to manhood, and it may be therefore that he has in mind the putting on of the *toga* of manhood by which a youth in the Greco-Roman world marked the change in everyday life. The believer "puts on" Christ, accepts the responsibilities and privileges of sonship; becomes a fellow citizen with God's saints: and all that is Christ's becomes his.

In this new standing human distinctions have no place. A Jewish prayer of a later date, but which might nevertheless have its origin in earlier times, ran: "My God, I thank thee that I was not born a Gentile, but a Jew; not a slave but a free man; not a woman but a man". How foolish are human boastings and human distinctions! None of these classifications has any value in Christ—there is neither Jew nor Greek, bond nor free, male nor female. All human categories, whether of race, of social status, or of sex, assume their insignificant place within God's purpose. All become "one" in Christ Jesus: for all men and women, whatever their distinction of race or class, are lifted up to the higher state of participation in the divine unity which is His purpose with man. We looked at the "unity" in considering verses 16 and 20. We now see it to be nothing less than inclusion in God's family of redeemed sons: one with Him through the exalted Redeemer, the Son of God. The theme is in this phase rounded off and related to the subject that has run throughout chapter 3 by the concluding words: "And if ye be Christ's, then are ye Abraham's seed, and heirs according to the promise" (verse 29).

## THE PLACE OF THE LAW ILLUSTRATED BY HUMAN LAW (4:1–7)

ALTHOUGH chapter 4 continues the argument by which Paul would regain the Galatians from their danger of lapsing to Judaism, since the chapter division tends to break the connection it may be well to sum up briefly at this point the argument of chapter 3. At his visit Paul had vividly portrayed Christ as a crucified Saviour, and on their acceptance of this preaching they had received the confirming gifts of the Spirit. The preacher had based his whole case upon faith as the operative power in his own life and also in theirs. This conformed to the classic illustration in Scripture—the case of Abraham in Genesis 15:6. Faith was the condition upon which men were united to Abraham and by which in fact they were counted as his sons. The testimony of Scripture was that faith and not works was the one human contribution to justification—for himself man could do nothing; he must receive what God had provided.

While the blessing came by faith, the Law brought a curse because of human frailty and inability to keep the requirements of Law. Hence the very subjects of Law needed redemption from it, and even this was provided in Christ. In Christ, then, the promises were centred; through him they would be fulfilled, and therefore also in him was to be found the unifying principle by which God would bring men to be "one" with Himself. The Law was a temporary measure holding men in guard. This marked it as belonging to an earlier stage of human life, to the time of childhood. Law belongs to childhood; faith to manhood. The Law ended with the coming of Christ, the exemplar of faith—and the preaching of the gospel brought to men an invitation to become sons of God, not slaves of law. Since sonship is based upon faith, and the principle of faith has been in Scripture linked essentially with Abraham and the promises made to him, such sonship is also heirship of the promises to Abraham. Christ is "the seed"; by faith they become children of God; they attain to heirship.

## The Saints as Heirs

The word *heir* of 3:29 is the connecting link with the next verse, 4:1, where Paul cites the illustration in human law of the temporary submission of the heir of an estate to servants. There must be training and discipline to fit any man for the responsibilities that fall to him in adult life, and the training in its length and severity corresponds to the responsibility to be assumed. It was even so in God's arrangements. The period of law was the time of training and discipline preparatory to something to be bestowed.

To guard against mistake it may be well to emphasise that Paul is only giving an illustration which broadly fits the matter. He is looking at the long sweep of history and comparing all of it with its changing institutions to the lifetime of a man, with its years of childhood followed by manhood. The long period of the law was comparable to a tutelage—the gospel period to the developed stage of faith. But this does not mean that no individuals of the Mosaic age reached saving faith. There were a few under the law who, seeing its limited place as a national code, looked to sharing a future by faith. The law was national, faith is individual; and Paul is thinking of national life, embracing its citizens in its orbit of law. To argue from Paul's illustration either that all who had lived under law were excluded from faith, or that conversely all would grow up to the faith and standing of heirs with the freedom which belongs to it, would reduce his illustration to absurdity.

Verses 1 and 2 present a clear correspondence with verses 3 and 4. We quote verses 1 and 2 using italic type for the essential words to which a parallel will be found in verses 3 and 4:

"Now I say, That the *heir*, as long as he is a *child*, differeth nothing from a *servant*, though he be lord of all; but is under *tutors and governors* until the *time appointed* of the father."

The child, whatever his future position may be, is for practical purposes like a slave: he is under the direction of guardians who look after his person, and stewards who have charge of the administration of property and affairs: such conditions last for the length of time arranged by the father.

Verses 3 and 4 read: "Even so we, when we were *children*, were in *bondage* under the *elements of the world*: but when

77

*the fulness of the time* was come, God sent forth his Son, made of a woman, made under the law". Mark the recurrence of the words "child" (verse 2), "children" (verse 3): "servant" or "slave" (verse 1) corresponds to "bondage" (verse 3); the "guardians and stewards" of verse 2 are the "elements of the world"; the "time appointed" of verse 2 is parallel to the "fulness of time" (verse 4). Nearly all these features are recalled in the "allegory" by which Paul concludes this section of his argument in 4:21–31.

When Paul says "we"—"when we were children"—he means the Jewish people of which he was a member. How fully he had known the restraints of law! But how much more he now understood the purpose of it, and enjoyed his present freedom! The elements, or rudiments of the world, are the simple beginnings, as the letters of the alphabet are the beginnings of learning. The external rites and ceremonies of the law were the elements of instruction but not an end in themselves; but subjection to them was essential until the realities in Christ which they foreshadowed were come. The fulness of time suggests a measure slowly filling with the passing years, registering movement towards a crisis determined by the one who had provided the measure. The last grain ran into the vessel—the hour of change had come. We have before commented on Paul's "philosophy of history" in his words in 3:19: the same thought is to be found here in the words "the fulness of time".

The "coming of the seed" (3:19) was at the "fulness of the time". Then "God sent forth His Son". Twice before Paul has specifically referred to the Son of God. It had pleased God to reveal His Son in Paul when the crisis in Paul's life occurred on the way to Damascus (1:16); and Paul who had died to Law lived unto God "by the faith of the Son of God who", says Paul, "loved me and gave himself for me" (2:20). He has shown also that the principle of faith as the family bond among the "blessed" justified, involves adoption into Abraham's family, for children of faith become Abraham's children, God having made Abraham the "father of many nations". He has gone further, asserting that men and women by faith in Christ Jesus become "children of God" (3:26). The basis upon which they can become God's children must now be set forth. The climax of God's revelation of His grace concerns this fact—that men become sons of God; but that climax had to wait the crisis in history when God sent forth His Son.

## The Only Begotten Son

It is easy to speak of the birth of Jesus, and of the fact of his divine sonship; but it is not easy to apprehend the stupendousness of it—that for the purposes of man's redemption God begot a son of the human race. As the astonishment and reverence at the fact that "God was manifest in the flesh" in one who was "the Word made flesh" grows upon us, so we value aright the distinctive feature of New Testament revelation—that we are God's adopted sons in Jesus, the only begotten Son. The maturity of Dr. Thomas' grasp of the divine revelation is marked by the fact that he comprehended and so lucidly set out this doctrine of God-manifestation in *Eureka*, to which readers may be directed for fuller details (Vol. I: pages 87–115).

Paul states two facts in connection with the coming of the Son of God, and draws two corresponding consequences. But since he states them in what is called an introversion, a figure frequently used by the prophets and the Lord Jesus, we set out the facts and results in parallel. God sent forth His Son

"made (born RV) of a woman,
    made (born RV) under the law,
    to redeem them that were under the law,
that we might receive the adoption of sons."

Christ by birth sustained two relationships—he was a member of our race, and he was a Jew under the Law of Moses. These two relationships brought him into personal contact with the two great needs of men. Because he was under the Law, he could redeem those under law; because he was a son of man (though not a son of *a man*) he could redeem us from sin and death and reconcile us to God, and so bring us to sonship.

We have already considered the position of Christ in relation to the Law, when examining Paul's words in 3:13. Christ redeemed from the curse of the Law because he was himself made a curse in the mode of his death. To achieve this he must be under the Law and therefore must be born of a woman of Israel's race. The real significance of the fact that Christ was born under the Law would be better appreciated by Paul than by us, for Paul knew what was involved in trying to live under the Law. The Law was not something detached—a matter merely for theological discussion—the Law was there to be obeyed, and to the earnest man oppressively there. For its curse to be removed and for the law itself to be taken away was an unspeakable relief; for the Law not only declared the will of God, but for all under it, it connoted the condemnation of God. To say then that Christ was born under the Law, was to say that he was born in such a relationship to the existing appointments of God that the burden of the Law could be carried by him, that the curse could fall upon him and yet he could be saved out of death by the glory of the Father, and thus men, cursed by the Law for their transgressions, could yet be redeemed.

"Born of a woman" proclaims a wider relationship than "born under the law". The latter is limited to Jews—the former is universal. The divine redemption was designed to meet the needs of all and all their needs.

There is something in the combined phrases "*sent forth* His Son", and "*born* of a woman" that marks out the Saviour as the Son of God. The divine origin is not only in the fact that God "sent forth", nor yet simply in the clear statement that Christ is called His Son, but as though to weave a three-fold cord Paul says that Jesus was "made" of a woman (RV "born"),using a word that means "he came to be". Why does he use that, rather unusual, word here when later in the chapter (4:29), speaking of Abraham's son, he is content to use the common word for human birth? The virgin birth is an adequate explanation, and perhaps the only adequate explanation, of Paul's choice of the word he uses.

The divine sonship of Jesus being thus forcefully indicated, we can perceive the significance of the phrase which expresses the result of his coming. He was made under the law to redeem those under law, but made the Son of God that men might be adopted as sons of God. The relationship (son) was more important than the condition (under the law), and the result is greater too. It could be said that he vas born of a woman to redeem us from the bondage of sin and death. But Paul declares a positive fact which embraces that redemption; Jesus was the Son of God, and in his birth we have the beginning of a divine family: it was God's purpose that he should "be the firstborn among many brethren" (Romans 8:29).

As we have said, in this phase of apostolic teaching we have the climax of divine revelation, which was progressive in form, corresponding to the circumstances which occasioned each part of the unfolding purpose. When at last the Redeemer was born, long promised in all God's "many ways and many parts" of Old Testament revelation, then it was proclaimed that through the Son of God men could become sons of God. To as many as believed on his name gave he power to become sons of God (John 1:12). Such may be implicit in Old Testament promises of everlasting life, but its explicit declaration was associated with the manifestation of the only begotten Son of God. Through him men receive "the adoption of sons".

## Adopted as Sons

The process of adoption is not without some analogy to the "sending forth" of the Son of God. Divine begettal is declared of both; in the fullest, completest sense, even of his bodily existence, in the case of Jesus; but of the "new man" formed within the sons of men, of the mental and moral renewal through the word, in the case of the adopted sons. "Of his own will begat he us" (James 1:18); or in Paul's words: "We are his workmanship, created in Christ Jesus unto good works" (Ephesians 2:10). It is interesting to observe that in the address given to the Galatian readers when Paul first visited them this double reference occurs. "To you is the word of this salvation sent"—God had sent forth the Word—and it is probable that here (as in Hebrews 4:12) the Word has a double significance, the message preached and he whom the message proclaimed—the word made flesh, to whom Paul applies the words of Psalm 2:7: "Thou art my son, this day have I begotten thee" (Acts 13:26,33).

"The adoption of sons" brings kinship to the Son; hence he declares that "he is not ashamed to call them brethren" (Hebrews 2:11). But he rejoices in the brotherhood with them, not because of some legal change, but because, being "reborn", they have the family likeness; and the fact of sonship—"because ye are sons"—is seen, says Paul, in that "God hath sent forth the spirit of his Son into your hearts, crying Abba, Father" (verse 6). We must mark the parallel: God sent forth His Son into the world: God sent forth the spirit of His Son into our hearts. The source in both cases is of God—the medium through which divine energy is manifested may differ. By the operative power of the Holy Spirit the Son was sent forth; by the power of the Spirit-word the spirit of Christ is fashioned in men. Because it is the life of Christ that is revealed in the believer, it is a life of dependence on God, of fellowship with God, of obedience to God, of service to God. And as the Son continually sought the Father in prayer, so do the sons of God. In fact, this feature of prayer to God with the associated idea that there is an open way of approach, is dominant in the thought of Paul here. This may be seen when we look carefully at the gospels and observe how Jesus uses the words "Father", "My Father", "O Righteous Father". Because of his unique relationship to God he uses the first person *"My* Father". But none but he can so speak. All other sons of God share an adoption in which none has priority; hence to them Jesus taught the prayer, *"Our* Father". In the use of this prayer, rightly apprehended, the believer remembers that his right of approach is not an exclusive possession, nor yet one of personal right. He is one of a family, redeemed by the Son of God, and as one of the family, privileged to use the filial token which others share, in the words "Our Father". The expression in Galatians 4:6, like its parallel in Romans 8:15, is undoubtedly a reference to what is called the Lord's Prayer. It is the Lord's prayer in that he gave it, but it is the disciple's prayer for use.

The use of the same double term "Abba, Father", here and in Romans 8, is itself sufficient to suggest that the same theme is to be found in both places. Romans is the amplification of Galatians on this as on other matters dealt with in the two epistles. The word "spirit" has beclouded many a controversy, when attention to meaning and usage would have allowed the brightness and beauty of divine light to shine from it. A series of contrasted terms runs through the letter to the Romans from 7:7 to 8:17—good and evil, spiritual and carnal, the inner man and the outer man, the law of the mind and the law of the flesh, an "I" which is now one and now the other, the flesh and the spirit. Three terms are equated in Romans 8:10 which should make the usage clear: "If the spirit of God dwell in you", "If any man have not the spirit of Christ", "If Christ be in you". The spirit in this context is at once God's spirit, Christ's spirit, and Christ in us. Where God's spirit and Christ's spirit is, then "ye are not in the flesh but in the spirit"; even though as in Paul's case there is the groaning cry, "Who shall deliver me from this body of death?" (Romans 7:25).

The sending forth of God's spirit being a proof, and the language of the very prayer being witness, it is confirmed they were now sons. "So that (RV) thou art *no more* a servant, but a son; and if a son, then an heir of God through Christ". "No more": they could not go back to the bondage—the seducers made a false appeal, the experience of sonship made hollow the call to slavery: only depraved sons lapsed to servitude. But sons alert and alive to the privilege of sonship recognise that sonship carries heirship, and the thought, passing through the illustration of minors as bondslaves to the development of sons, circles to the starting point of heirship: "heir according to the promise" (3:29); "heirs of God through Christ" (4:7).

## DANGER OF GOING BACK (4:8–11)

THE RV punctuation of verses 8 and 9 shows that the connection of the first word "Howbeit" is with "turning back", verse 9. The RV reads as follows: "Howbeit at that time, not knowing God, ye were in bondage to them which by nature are no gods: but now that ye have come to know God, or rather to be known of God, how turn ye back again to the weak and beggarly rudiments, whereunto ye desire to be in bondage over again?"

A sad contrast is evident in these verses with the glowing language concerning sonship of the earlier verses. In view of the glorious facts connected with the gospel of God's grace, how could they turn again to that from which they have been delivered? They had been as Gentiles without God, and were enslaved to forms of worship which were no gods. In nothing is the folly of idolatry more evident than in its futility. The gods worshipped do not possess the qualities and powers ascribed to them, but are endowed with attributes that only exist in the mind of the worshipper. Whatever was in the idol was due to the idol-maker, but no craftsman could endue an image with divinity. Scorchingly Hosea declares: "The workman made it; therefore it is not God, but the calf of Samaria shall be broken in pieces" (8:6). The ignorance of idolatry had been replaced in the minds of the Galatians by the knowledge of the true God. This is obviously the inevitable first step in salvation. There must be recognition of the Almighty—that He is the Almighty, that He is high and holy, just and true, loving and forbearing. We cannot know this unless God reveals Himself and, even so, our understanding of the revelation is not an occasion of glorying. For there is another aspect, more vital, yet related: the knowledge man has acquired is not of his initiative, for not only has the revealed word come from God, but its very operation upon men is of God. Thus man is humbled and fitted for the elevating thought that he is "known of God". Within that expression lies also the deeper thought, not merely that God is aware of the man, but that God recognises the man. In this sense Paul says: "If any man love God, the same is known of him" (1 Corinthians 8:3).

In turning to Judaism, the Galatians were turning to elemental alphabetic things—which Paul calls "the weak beggarly rudiments"—to be enslaved again thereby.

The principles of law with its enactments and its ritual, largely concerned with externals, belong to the elementary. The Law was weak in that it is powerless to give men life or fellowship with God: it was beggarly in its poverty when compared with the riches of God's glory in Christ Jesus His Son. Now Paul describes a turn to Judaism as a return, a going back, although it is evident that their former ways of life were in no way connected with the Mosaic law. In what way is there such a parallel between their old pagan ways that turning to the ritual of the Law was to them a returning? Obviously, Paul cannot be thinking there was no difference between the great things of God's law, holy, just and good, and the base, depraved ideas and ceremonies of nature worship. The resemblance is in the effect upon the worshipper. Both enslaved to forms of law; both dealt with elementary things; both were weak in their influence upon the worshipper; neither, as a result, had anything to offer that had abiding worth. Law, as well as pagan practices, led to self-centredness, with the interest fixed on man's works; neither gave the experience of God that comes by faith.

Ramsay has described the Phrygian ritual in his book, *Cities and Bishoprics of Phrygia*, in the following words:

"A highly elaborate religious system reigned over the country. Superstitious devotion to an artificial system of rules, and implicit obedience to the directions of the priests, were universal among the uneducated native population. The priestly hierarchy at the great religious centres expounded the will of God to his worshippers. Thus the government was a theocracy, and the whole system, with its prophets, priests, religious law, punishments inflicted by the God for infractions of the ceremonial law, warnings and threats, and the set of superstitious minutiae, presented a remarkable and real resemblance in external type to the old Jewish ceremonial and religious rule. It is not until this is properly apprehended that Galatians 4:3–11 becomes clear and natural. Paul in that message implies that the Judaizing movement of the Christian Galatians is a recurrence to their old heathen type. After being set free from the bonds of a hard ceremonial law, they were putting themselves once more into the bonds of another ceremonial law, equally hard. In their action they were showing themselves senseless (Galatians 3:1), devoid of the educated mind that could perceive the real nature of things. There is an intentional emphasis in the juxtaposition of 'senseless' with 'Galatian' for it was the more educated party, opposed to the native superstition, that would most warmly welcome the provincial title. Hence the address 'senseless Galatians', already anticipates the longer expostulation (4:3–11), 'Galatians who are sinking from the educated standard to the ignorance and superstition of the native religion'."

Luther, upon whom this epistle had such an influence, and through whom a revolution in the religious world took place in consequence, discerned the resemblance. We quote literally from the English translation of Luther's *Commentary* on Galatians published in 1644:

"But why saith Paul that the Galatians turned back again to weak and beggarly rudiments or ceremonies, that is to say, to the law, whereas, they never had the law? for they were Gentiles (not withstanding he wrote these things to the Jews also, as afterwards we will declare) or why speaketh he not rather after this manner? Once when ye knew not God, ye did service unto them which by nature were no gods: but now seeing ye know God, why turne ye backe againe, forsaking the true God to worship Idols? Doth Paul take it to be all one thing, to fall from the promise to the law, from faith to works, and to doe service unto Gods which by nature are no gods? I answer: Whosoever is fallen from the article of Justification, is ignorant of God, and an Idolater. Therefore it is all one thing whether he afterwards turn againe to the law, or to worshipping of idols: it is all one, whether he be called a Monke, a Turke, a Jew, or an Anabaptist. For when this Article is taken away, there remaineth nothing else but errour, hypocrisie, impiety and Idolatry, how much soever it seem in outward appearance to be the very truth, the true service of God, and true holiness.

"The reason is, because God will or can be knowne no otherwise than by Christ, according to that saying of John 1. The onely begotten Sonne which is in the bosome of the Father, hee hath declared him. He is the Seede promised unto Abraham, in whom God hath established all his promises. Wherefore Christ is the onely meane, and as ye would say, the glasse by the which we see God, that is to say, we know his will. For in Christ we see that God is not a cruell exactour or a judge, but a most favourable, loving and mercifull Father, who to the end he might blesse us, that is to say, deliver us from the law, sinne, death and all evils, and might endue us with grace, righteousnesse and everlasting life, spared not his owne Sonne, but gave him for us all. This is a true knowledge of God, and a divine perswasion, which deceiveth us not, but painteth out God unto us lively.

"He that is fallen from this knowledge, must needs conceive this fantasie in his heart: I will set up such a service of God: I will enter into such an order: I will chuse this or that work, and so will I serve God, and I doubt not but God will accept this, and reward me with everlasting life for the same. For he is mercifull and liberall, giving all good things even to the unworthy and unthankfull, much more will he give unto me grace and everlasting life for my great and manifold good deeds and merits. This is the highest wisdome, righteousnesse and religion that reason can judge of: which is common to all nations, to the Papists, Jews, Turkes, Heretickes, etc. They can go no higher than that Pharisee did, of whom mention is made in the Gospell. They have no knowledge of the Christian righteousnes, or of the righteousnes of faith. For the naturall man perceiveth not the mysteries of God. Also: There is none that understandeth, there is none that seeketh after God. Therefore there is no difference at all betweene a Papist, a Jew, a Turke and a Hereticke. Indeed there is a difference of the persons, the places, rites, religions, works and worshippings: notwithstanding there is all one and the same reason, the same heart, opinion and cogitation in them all. For the Turke thinketh the self-same thing that the Charter-house Monke doth: namely if I doe this or that worke, God will be mercifull unto me: If I doe it not, he will be angry. There is no meane between mans working and the knowledge of Christ. If this knowledge be darkened or defaced, it is all one whither thou be a Monke, a Turke, a Jew."

"I am afraid of you" Paul said: not just for you, but of you: their action in turning to the observance of days and festivals filled him with dread that his labour would be all in vain.

PERSONAL APPEAL BASED UPON MUTUAL EXPERIENCE
(4:12–20)

THE emotion of Paul is perhaps nowhere more evident than in this epistle. Earnestness, zeal, anxiety, strong opposition to those who were undoing his work are all seen, and with it all we feel with the man. The dread of failure in his work among them leads him with deep affection to appeal to them, recalling his visit, his circumstances and their response. "I beseech you, brethren, be as I am, for I was like you." When he and Barnabas were with them they practised no legal observances, observed no feasts. They were messengers bringing God's grace to them. They had known the Law and had been in bondage to it, but when they came to Galatia with the gospel, they were as free from the Law as the Galatians themselves. "Be as I am"—join me in my stand on faith in Christ crucified and risen.

This section of the epistle is very personal in tone, and this fact helps us to recognise an allusiveness that might otherwise be overlooked. We have previously seen that Paul refers to communications from them to himself; and also we may see a reference to words they had used to him. "Ye did me no wrong"—the RV probably catches up an expression used by the Galatians. They may have so said by way of explaining why they had modified their ways. "You *did* not", Paul takes up, "but now you do. You did not then, but everything otherwise. Let us recall how you received me", and he reminds them of the physical disability from which he suffered when among them—a disability of a kind which normally would have been regarded as a divine retribution; but instead of despising him they had received him as a divine messenger. In their joy they would have given him their eyes, so ready were they to give their dearest things.

What was the illness from which Paul suffered when in Galatia? Clearly complete proof for any theory is not possible, and many explanations have been advanced. It is natural to associate with this reference to his illness the other reference in 2 Corinthians 12:7 where he speaks of the thorn in the flesh, and to find in both allusion to the same trouble. From the reference to the eyes a view widely held has identified his sickness with acute eye trouble, possibly an after effect of the blindness caused by the meeting with the glorified Lord on the way to Damascus. Lewin in his *Paul* has put this case perhaps as well as any writer.

Ramsay has advocated another explanation which has very much to commend it. In his *Paul, the Traveller* he argues that it was an illness that led Paul and Barnabas to go to Antioch. Ramsay says:

"In passing from Perga to Pisidian Antioch, the travellers passed from the Roman province Pamphylia to the Roman province Galatia, and the rest of their journey lay in Galatia until they returned to Perga. Now, we possess a letter written by Paul to the Churches of Galatia, in which he says: 'Ye know that it was by reason of physical infirmity that I preached the Gospel unto you on the first of my two visits; and the facts of my bodily constitution which were trying to you were not despised nor rejected by you, but ye received me as a messenger of God'. We learn, then,

87

from Paul himself that an illness (we may confidently say a serious illness) was the occasion of his having originally preached to the churches of Galatia. The words do not necessarily imply that the illness began in Galatia; they were quite consistent with the interpretation that the illness was the reason why he came to be in Galatia and had the opportunity of preaching there; but they imply that the physical infirmity lasted for some considerable time, and was apparent to strangers, while he was in Galatia.

"Here we have a reason, stated by Paul himself, which fully explains all the curious phenomena of the text of Acts. Paul had a serious illness in Pamphylia and on that account he left Perga and went to Antioch. It is unnecessary to repeat the argument that this is in perfect agreement with the known facts. Any constitutional weakness was liable to be brought out by 'the sudden plunge into the enervating atmosphere of Pamphylia' after the fatigue and hardship of a journey on foot through Cyprus, accompanied by the constant excitement of missionary work, culminating in the intense nervous strain of the supreme effort at Paphos. The natural and common treatment for such an illness is to go to the higher ground of the interior; and the situation of Antioch (about 3,600 feet above the sea, sheltered by mountains on the north and east, and overlooking a wide plain to the south and south-west), as well as its Jewish population, and commercial connection with the Pamphylian coast-cities, made it a very suitable place for Paul's purpose."

Ramsay also suggests that an intermittent malaria was the "thorn in the flesh". He says:

"The character of the Pamphylian country not merely in its modern half-cultivated condition, but at all times, must have been enervating and calculated to bring out any latent weakness of constitution. Now it is a probable and generally accepted view that the 'physical weakness' which was the occasion why Paul preached to the Galatians, was the same malady which tormented him at frequent intervals. I have suggested that this malady was a species of chronic malaria fever; and, in view of criticisms, it is necessary to dwell on this point; for I have incurred the blame of exaggerating an ephemeral attack. The question is put whether such an illness 'could reasonably have called forth their contempt and loathing'.

88

"A physical weakness, which recurs regularly in some situation that one is regularly required by duty to face, produces strong and peculiar effect on our human nature ...

"Now, in some constitutions malaria fever tends to recur in very distressing and prostrating paroxysms, whenever one's energies are taxed for a great effort. Such an attack is for the time absolutely incapacitating: the sufferer can only lie and feel himself a shaking and helpless weakling, when he ought to be at work. He feels a contempt and loathing for self, and believes that others feel equal contempt and loathing."

There appears to be some evidence from inscriptions that malaria was regarded in ancient times as being a penalty sent by God. The recurring paroxysms seemed to be directly due to divine act. If such a view was held by the Galatians, it gives strong point to Paul's statement that they did "not despise nor reject my physical infirmity, but received me as an angel of God". They did the opposite from what might have been expected, but so doing they judged rightly. Added to this, the malarial headache has been described by a sufferer as like "a red hot bar thrust through the forehead".

Efforts have been made to explain Paul's illness as epilepsy, and certain parallels have been suggested with prominent leaders who were known to be epileptics—Julius Caesar, Napoleon, Cromwell. The sceptic is predisposed to this explanation as "visions" are a feature of this complaint, and Paul's visions are thus regarded as the product of illness.

One difference between Paul and these others, however, is fatal to the comparison. Paul attributed his position, his power, his commission to the meeting with the risen Christ. The epileptic never finds in his weakness the basis of his particular genius. In addition, pain is not a feature of epilepsy, and whatever Paul's malady may have been it is clear that pain was a distressing feature from which Paul would have been free had his Lord willed it. Epilepsy is sometimes associated with the mental instability which marks some men of genius, and Paul's critics have not been slow to attribute insanity to him. But Ramsay's words in *Pauline Studies* are sound and just:

"The view that Paul's experience on the way to Damascus was due to some form of madness has been widely maintained in recent years. It is tacitly held by many who shrink from explicitly formulating it to their own mind. It is openly and resolutely declared by many learned and honest men. Scientific investigators have discussed and given a name to the precise class of madness to which Paul's delusions must be assigned.

"Now there have been many madmen in all times; but the difficulty which many feel in classing Paul among them arises from the fact that not merely did he persuade every one who heard him that he was sane and spoke the truth, but that also he had moved the world, changed the whole course of history, and made us what we are. Is the world moved at the word of a lunatic? To think so would be to abandon all belief in the existence of order and unity in the world and in history; and therefore we are driven to the conclusion that Paul's vision is one of the things about which evidence ought to be scrutinised and examined without any foregone conclusion in one's mind ...

"It must, therefore, be true that God reveals Himself to man in some way or other. Paul claims to have received such revelation; and we ought not to set aside his claim as irrational and necessarily false. Many such claims can easily be put away; but history has decided that his case is one which deserves scrutiny, examination, rigid testing."

The phrase in verse 15: "Where is then the blessedness ye spake of?" in the AV is obscure. The RV, "Where then is that gratulation of yourselves?" puts us on the track of understanding. They had received the truth with joy, regarding themselves as blessed in the favour now theirs. This response to the gospel message manifested itself in a gratitude to Paul for which no sacrifice was too great—even the eyes, the most precious of possessions, would have been given for Paul's sake.

This "gratulation" had evidently passed with the new teaching, and with it had gone also the love for Paul. They felt he was not a true friend—it may be that Paul is catching hold of his opponents' description of him when he uses the word "enemy". "Am I therefore become your enemy because I tell you the truth?" or "deal truly with you?" It was said that while claiming to bring them the gospel, he had brought an incomplete and futile message—that was really an enemy's work; so the Judaizers suggested. Was the trouble he had taken, however, that of an "enemy"? he asks. Is "dealing truly" with men an "enemy action"? The Judaizers paid court to them; they did not speak the truth but, pretending a warm interest in the Galatians, they nevertheless did "not do well". They would exclude—or "they desire to shut you out" (verse 17, RV); they taught that they were excluded from salvation apart from observing the Law. This they did that the Galatians "may seek (RV) them".

Paul's attention to them was personally disinterested: he would that someone was with them always, and always "zealously affected" towards them, providing it was for good. He would not have them dependent upon him; it did not matter who ministered to them so long as it was sincere and for their good. But there is implied the fact that the teachers who had been mischievously working in their midst were not doing them good, and Paul's feelings find expression in the vivid figure of travail—he had laboured to bring them to their birth in Christ, and he now felt the pangs of anguish for them as he suffers to bring them back to the liberty of sons of God. He longed to be with them, no longer admonishing and arguing the truth, but with changed voice happy in the harmony of God's good news. "I long ... for I am perplexed about you" (RV), or as the same words in a papyrus scrap appear to mean, "I am at my wits' end".

## AN ALLEGORY (4:21–31)

AFTER the moving appeal to loyalty to the gospel Paul had preached to the Galatians, the apostle reverts to the question of the Law and the bondservice which it imposed upon those who tried to keep it. The comparison he has before made of the position during childhood of an heir with that of a slave, suggests the history of two sons of different status in patriarchal times. The lives of Ishmael and Isaac are shown to contain an allegorical representation of God's purpose in the Law and in the gospel. "Tell me, ye that desire to be under the law", he begins, "do ye not hear the law?" First we note the description and use of Scripture. The Law which he would have them hear is not some legal enactment of Leviticus, but biography from the book of Genesis. This book was the first of the five books which together were called the Law in the threefold division of the Old Testament then current. The same book is "the scripture" of verse 30, and a citation from it is prefaced by the words "It is written". Such a style of citation implies an unquestioning faith in the history to be used by way of argument.

Abraham had two sons by two mothers. One woman was a bondslave given to the husband as a slave-wife because of the barrenness of the true wife, who was a princess. Later by a divine miracle a child was born to the wife. In the consequent developments the insubordinate wildness of the bondslave's

91

child was manifested, leading to the casting out of both
mother and child. Paul works out the allegory in some detail
which might be first shown in diagrammatic form. The two
women represented two covenants, two mountains, two cities,
and there are two sons; the circumstances of the mothers and
sons are shown to have a significance, all together forming
one consistent lesson.

| TWO | HAGAR | SARAH |
|---|---|---|
| women | bondslave | free woman—princess |
| mountains | Sinai in Arabia | Zion in land of promise |
| covenants | from Sinai—the letter that killeth—bringing forth slaves. | from Zion—the spirit that gives life—bringing forth sons |
| cities | Jerusalem that "now is" (in Paul's day) | Jerusalem to come |
| sons | born after the flesh—a persecutor—cast out | born after spirit—persecuted—heirs of God |

The episode as a whole as recorded in Genesis is in keeping with the customs of patriarchal times, as reflected in the
law of Khammurabi (thought to be the Amraphel of Genesis
14:1, but in the fluctuating opinions of archaeologists now
doubted by some). The law of this Babylonian ruler was in
operation to the western sea boundary of the Middle East;
and among other regulations forbad the disinheriting of a
concubine's son in favour of the later-born son of the true
wife. When Abram pleaded that Ishmael might be the heir he
was conforming to this law by recognising the heirship of
Ishmael. But divine law overstepped human law, and
Ishmael was not allowed to be the seed.

The operative cause in the birth of the two sons involves a
divine rule. The flesh was sufficient for the production of
Ishmael, and on the principle that like produces like, fleshly
ways very clearly revealed themselves in Ishmael's life.

Salvation must be by regeneration, and since man is
unable to redeem himself, the means of regeneration must
come from God. This is seen in every stage of the work. We
see it in the birth of the Saviour who was the Word made
flesh; we see it in his resurrection by the glory of the Father,
by which he became the word of life; in fact, the whole process
is expressed in the apostolic phrase, "God was in Christ reconciling the world unto himself". There is an analogy to this

work of the spirit in the firstborn in the way "many sons" are being "brought unto glory". The word of God is the formative agent under the over-ruling providence of God: "Of his own will begat he us by the word of truth that we might be a kind of firstfruits of his creatures" (James 1:18). The word continues to be the guiding and moulding instrument throughout the life of probation. Throughout the whole process is God's creative energy. "By grace are ye saved through faith; and that not of yourselves: it is the gift of God: not of works, lest any man should boast. For we are his workmanship, created in Christ Jesus unto good works, which God hath before ordained that we should walk in them" (Ephesians 2:8–10).

Paul does not hesitate to state side by side the two factors indispensable to a man's salvation but which to human reasoning can appear to be incompatibles: "Wherefore ... work out your own salvation with fear and trembling; for it is God which worketh in you both to will and to do of his good pleasure" (Philippians 2:12,13). And lest this operation of God should lead to fatalism he adds, "Do all things without murmurings and disputings". When man has done his part in accepting God's grace and abjuring sin, the final transformation to the likeness of Christ's body of glory is effected by the working of that energy "whereby he is able even to subdue all things unto himself" (Philippians 3:21).

In the allegory the regenerative action of God was seen in the birth of the Seed promised to Abraham. "By faith even Sarah herself received power to conceive seed when she was past age" (Hebrews 11:11, RV). Nor was the miracle confined to Sarah, for Paul also says, "And being not weak in faith, he considered not his own body now dead, when he was about an hundred years old, neither yet the deadness of Sarah's womb: he staggered not at the promise of God through unbelief; but was strong in faith, giving glory to God; and being fully persuaded that, what he had promised, he was able also to perform" (Romans 4:19–21).

Paul therefore can say that "the child by promise"—who was therefore foreseen by God and included in His purpose—was "born after the spirit". Flesh and spirit, man and God, are the sources of the two children of Abraham. In this, as in all parts of God's dealings with men, that is first which is natural and afterwards that which is spiritual. First Ishmael, then a long wait of fourteen years during which all natural hope receded, and at last when it was clear that only God's power could achieve His purpose, Isaac was born. While the Jewish race thus owe their origin to a miracle of begettal, this does not make the nation into "the Seed", for they are all flesh-born sons of Isaac and Jacob, and as a nation reject the antitype of Isaac. The life of Isaac, in birth, in offering, in restoration, is a parable of "the Seed" through whom the promise will be made effective.

The two covenants may be described as the Abrahamic and the Mosaic, although the reason for the names being thus attached are not the same in both cases. Abraham himself received God's covenant; Moses mediated God's covenant with Israel. The one was individual in its application; the other national. The individual concerned the everlasting inheritance of the land, and therefore the bestowal of ever-lasting life: the national concerned the occupation of the land by the nation subject to continued obedience. The Abrahamic, in keeping with the rule "afterwards that which is spiritual", is the last to be effective, and still awaits a future day for its realisation. The Mosaic, being the first in operation, and hav-ing completed its purpose in apostolic times, is called "the old covenant", while the Abrahamic is called the "new covenant".

## The New Covenant

Fundamental to the "new", since it confers a title to everlast-ing life, is the forgiveness of sins. The "old covenant" with its repeated sacrifices could not make perfect them that drew nigh to God. The one offering able to do this is the sacrifice of Jesus Christ: "We are sanctified through the offering of the body of Jesus Christ once for all" (Hebrews 10:10). Hence Jesus said of the memorial wine: "This is the blood of the new covenant, shed for many for the remission of sins" (Matthew 26:28). This statement of Jesus is verbally linked with two important Old Testament prophecies. Jeremiah, contempo-rary with the overthrow of the Kingdom, foretells the regath-ering and the rebuilding of their national life. The old covenant had been broken by Israel, but God would initiate them when regathered into a new covenant which would con-trast with the old in several particulars. The law given through Moses was written on tables of stone, fit symbol of the stony hearts of Israel, unresponsive to God's will. Under the new covenant God will write His laws on their hearts, and men will know God. Under this new covenant God "will forgive their iniquity, and will remember their sin no more". This very fact involves that the conditions for forgiveness must have been established, and therefore identifies beyond doubt the new covenant of Jeremiah's prophecy with that confirmed in the Lord's shed blood. When Israel are regath-ered they will individually be acceptable to God—the rebels will have been purged out, and all who enter the land will "call upon the name of the Lord", recognising that in Mount Zion there is deliverance. The Redeemer will have come to Zion and turned away transgression from Jacob, who on their part will turn to the Lord, the veil that covers their heart at present having been removed.

"Shed for *many*", Jesus said of the cup which was the emblem of the blood of the new covenant. It is only one word, but the allusion is recognised by careful students as a reference to the prophecy of the Lord's servant, who would pour out his soul unto death as an offering for sin, and of whom God said: "By his knowledge shall my righteous servant justify *many*" (Isaiah 53:11).

The importance and superiority of the new covenant are dealt with in Hebrews, chapters 8 to 10, the prophecy of Jeremiah chapter 31 being the starting point and also the basis of most of the exposition of the chapters.

## Jerusalem: Past and Future

The two mountains are Sinai and Zion, but with Zion there is an involution of ideas. For Jerusalem is before us at two periods, the past and the future: and in the past, while the Law of Moses was in force in the land, Jerusalem was in Paul's allegory associated with Sinai: "This Hagar is Mount Sinai in Arabia, and answereth to Jerusalem which now is, and is in bondage with her children." Jerusalem under the Mosaic covenant was represented by Sinai; both places were connected with the Law and owed their importance to it. Sinai was the place of the giving of the old covenant—and under that covenant Jerusalem was the city where the offerings required by the Law were made. When the Law was annulled the city shared the judgement upon the people. The cities of Palestine were laid waste when the people were carried away captives, and Jerusalem ceased to have her former importance religiously, nationally or internationally. A rival grew up on the seven hills by the Tiber, and for centuries men turned to Rome for guidance and instruction. It is a sign of a coming change that already the strategic importance of Palestine has returned. During the period when world-power, with Rome as its capital, encircled the Mediterranean, Palestine became marginal; but today, when the whole globe forms "the habitable", Palestine's importance is restored.

While the past estate of Jerusalem is linked with Sinai, her future will be on another foundation. God hath chosen Zion to put there *His name*, in the full Scriptural import of

95

the phrase. There the Lord has commanded the blessing even life for evermore. Her priests will be clothed with righteousness, the saints shout for joy; and parallel to this is a later verse: "I will also clothe her priests with salvation: and her saints shall shout aloud for joy" (Psalms 132:9,16; 133:3). Zion will then have a priest "made after the power of an endless life", one after the order of Melchizedec; and God will send the rod of his strength out of Zion (Psalm 110:2,4). When the branch of the Lord is revealed as "beautiful and glorious" (mark the language here of the high priestly clothing, Exodus 28:2,40), then "he that is left in Zion, and he that remaineth in Jerusalem, shall be called holy, even everyone that is written to life (margin) in Jerusalem" (Isaiah 4:3). "I will make thee", says God, "an eternal excellency, a joy of many generations", for men will call her "The city of the LORD, The Zion of the Holy One of Israel" (Isaiah 60:15,14). The prophets rise to sublime oratory in extolling this coming glory of the city of the Great King.

We have then Jerusalem in two periods of her history: first when she was the capital of God's Kingdom which was established on the basis of the Sinaitic covenant with Israel, when her charter was linked inseparably with the Arabian mountain of Sinai; and secondly—and this is still future—when she will be the throne of the Lord in a re-established kingdom with the Son of God and his saints in occupation, with a title conferred by God's covenant with Abraham—the covenant of everlasting life.

The two sons are related to the two mothers and are linked with their maternal status. The children of Jerusalem of the past were such under the law-covenant, and like Ishmael were bondslaves. "The law gendereth to bondage", and the Jews were enslaved by the law. The law of God given through Moses convicted them of sin, and in so doing revealed their thraldom to sin. All needed a deliverance, and this the law did not provide. Bondslaves have no title to permanence in a house, and Jews serving the Law (or ignoring it today but still enslaved to sin) are "to be cast out".

Sarah first spoke the words of rejection. When Isaac was weaned (he would be much older than the age of a child today when weaned, and Ishmael may have been seventeen), Sarah observed the son of Hagar mocking Isaac. This grieved her, and she demanded that he be "cast out". Abraham was very reluctant to comply, but he was instructed that such was the will of God: "Let it not be grievous in thy sight because of the lad, and because of thy bondwoman; in all that Sarah hath

96

said unto thee, hearken unto her voice, for in Isaac shall thy seed be called." Ishmael was rejected and Isaac was announced by God as the heir. This divine confirmation of Sarah's wishes gives her words Scriptural authority, and Paul quotes them prefaced with "What saith the scripture?"

Paul sees in Ishmael's mockery an illustration of the inevitable opposition of flesh to spirit. The same resentment was to be seen in the persecution of the Christians by the Jews. Even the apostatising activities which were perverting the Galatians were a manifestation of the Ishmael, law-enslaved spirit, and marked those Jews out as rejects and not heirs.

By contrast he rallies his readers to an appreciation of their high privileges. "Jerusalem which is above is free, which is the mother of us all." The reference to "above" does not mark the location of the heavenly city of which they were children. It is not "Jerusalem the golden" of the later doctrine of Christendom when the doctrine of the immortality of the soul had necessitated an abode for the departed. Jerusalem of the coming age is a heavenly city, with a heavenly consti-tution. In apocalyptic symbol her government, her munici-pality, is described as a foursquare city which descends from God. The "Lord from heaven", the last Adam, is her King. She is above, as the spiritual is higher than the fleshly, as immor-tality is higher than mortality, as a divinely enlightened people are higher than wayward, flesh-guided rebels.

The "mother of us all" is a beautiful figure, which had a powerful appeal to Paul. How touchingly he refers to Rufus, and "his mother and mine" (Romans 16:13). The weary trav-eller found rest and home with mother-comfort in the home of Rufus. So God through the prophet tenderly says: "As one whom his mother comforteth, so will I comfort you; and ye shall be comforted in Jerusalem" (Isaiah 66:13); and the context tells of "a nation born at once" to travailing Zion, a nation which the earth has been made to bring forth in one day, by resurrection (verses 7,8). A Psalm declares that "the Lord loveth the gates of Zion more than all the dwellings of Jacob. Glorious things are spoken of thee, O city of God" (87:2,3); and strangers from proud Gentile nations, having learned of God's intentions that He has "spoken" of the city, are represented as being enrolled as Zion's citizens. "This man was born there. Of Zion it shall be said, This and that man was born in her, and the highest himself shall establish her. The Lord shall count when he writeth up the people that this man was born there." Therefore Zion is their mother: and the LXX Version, with which Paul was familiar, reads: "Each shall call Zion, Mother! yea, each man was born in her." By the constraint that finds its compulsion in divine begettal by the word of God, men of faith are drawn to Jerusalem as their "mother city"; and Paul persuasively draws the Galatians to this as he closes his allegory: "So then, brethren, we are not children of the bondwoman, but of the free."

It is interesting to note that in the letter to the Hebrews an appeal is based upon the associations of Sinai and Zion. The handling of the theme is different, for the readers were so entirely unlike. But, believing as we do that Paul was the writer of both Galatians and Hebrews, we may observe the versatility shown in the way the same circumstances are used for exhortation. The essential difference is in the starting point—Galatians begins with Abraham's domestic affairs and works out the allegory by the parallel of the two mountains and the two women. In Hebrews the terrors of Sinai as the place where the law was given under conditions unbearable to those present, is contrasted with the joy shared by angels and men at the gathering in festal assembly in Zion of the justified in Christ, through his mediatorship of the new covenant.

# SECTION 4

## FAITH AND LIFE
### STAND FAST IN THE LIBERTY OF THE GOSPEL (5:1–12)

ALTHOUGH obscured a little by the chapter division the first verse of this chapter is clearly a link between what has been established in chapters 3 and 4, and that which follows. While some would treat the verse as concluding chapter 4, it really gathers up and then carries forward the conclusion. Paul says: "Stand fast therefore in the liberty wherewith Christ has made us free, and be not entangled again with the yoke of bondage." Itself exhortation— "stand fast"—it is also the start of the practical counsel based on the doctrines which have been established. "Christ has made us free" is a statement which should not be confined to narrow meanings. The freedom possible in Christ is a moral experience as well as an emancipation from legal enactments. The Roman world was enslaved to vice and lust; the Jewish world was little better, but Christian teaching, heartily and sincerely believed, was found to be a liberating power. It is true that there was also a freeing from the service to the Mosaic Law, but this is but a part of the deliverance. Additionally, there was potentially a release from the prison house to which sin hailed his captives—from death itself. This was indeed a freedom, such as belongs to the sons of the free woman (4:23,26,31), the sons of promise (4:23), the sons of God (4:29).

Freedom, rightly used, is a precious heritage. God has given man freedom to exercise his will, but has also given him laws to obey. Man in society finds it necessary to devise laws for the orderly arrangement of a communal life; but the task has tried his resources to the full and shown that to construct an ordered social life is beyond his power. To many liberty spells licence; and rule is a synonym for tyranny. On the other hand the corrupting influence of power over one's fellows is seen in the disordered state of many countries where a totalitarian form of government is established. Freedom for anything but unremitting toil is taken away from uncounted millions of men and women. Even in more favoured countries life is increasingly hedged about by regulations as the State and not the individual takes pride of place. The vigilance that

99

men must pay for freedom has itself been made impossible in many departments of life as the tentacles of the State have brought men within its grip.

Religious freedom has suffered with much else in many parts of the world—not for the first time. Bondage in this department of life has often come from devotees of religion, who have imposed ordinances and taken toll of human souls. Men can sometimes be enslaved bodily but have free souls; but no bondage is worse than that which fetters thought and worship.

There was a speciousness in the claim of the Judaizers that the Law was God-given. So it was; it was also taken away by God—He alone being able to do that. It had been taken away as a rule of life for men by the very act of obedience of Jesus Christ in his yielding to death, as the rent veil in the Temple showed. Such was the divinely arranged price of freedom. With Christ's sacrifice rightly understood in its relation to law, there could be no question about the duty of maintaining the freedom. If only that death of Christ could make free, then men should not seek to reimpose the law, and those delivered should avoid any further entanglement in a yoke which was bondage itself.

We have already noticed the underlying likeness between human ritual and the misused ritual of God. So these Galatians can be said to be entangled *again* if they surrendered their freedom to the Judaizers.

"Stand fast"—men ever seek to impose error for truth, slavery for sonship, the enmeshing regulation for the self-applied principle of action. So, though written for an Asia Minor group of believers enticed by a form of doctrine which belongs in outward form to a long past controversy, the principle holds good until men shall attain to the liberty of the glory of the sons of God (Romans 8:21).

There is an emphasis in the introduction of himself in verse 2: "Behold, I Paul say." Why is this? The answer is to be found in the perversion of his teaching by his opponents. 'He trims', they said; circumcision in Timothy's case, no circumcision of Titus: thus preaching circumcision when it suited him. He throws the charge back: "I, the one charged with being a preacher of the rite, tell you that if ye be circumcised, Christ shall profit you nothing." Observance of days, months and years, wrong as Paul has shown, was yet of minor significance compared with acceptance of circumcision. The rite is antithetic to the way of salvation in Christ. It is fleshly, implies a trust in the flesh and represents a trust in ritual and works that excludes faith. But faith is God's way—the only possible way—and faith is as exclusive as circumcision. There is no mid-way, where man can receive righteousness by faith and at the same time attain it by his own works. If, then, they turned to circumcision, Christ and his work could not profit; by their own act they had excluded Christ from their lives. The observance of the rite was a confession that for them faith was insufficient, and since faith has for its object Christ and his work, it also practically denied the Christ-way as adequate. Nothing remained but a full accept-ance of the old legal observance, futile and enslaving.

The assertion of verse 2 is enlarged and emphasised in verses 3 and 4, in a twofold statement. First the obligation which followed circumcision was nothing less than an absolute keeping of the whole law: to it he is a debtor, and from its penalties there was no escape. Second, it was a repu-diation of Christ: an act which cut them off from Christ. "Ye are *severed* from Christ" (RV)—a strong word found difficult to translate. "Struck with atrophy" is one paraphrase, sug-gesting an existence devoid of living power. Clearly this was so: seeking justification by law, they were fallen from grace; they were "cast forth" as Hagar was, as Paul suggests by repeating the word of 4:30. They had espoused an impossible way of justification and so failed to reach the true source of forgiveness and redemption. Law or grace; circumcision or Christ; they are exclusives and not complements. Choosing one they missed the other.

Circumcision was outward: it was of the flesh. A man's inner life was not thereby affected. Justification by faith had its base of operation in the mind, reforming and transform-ing. The end of the life begun in a cutting off of the flesh was the cutting off of life itself. The end of faith was righteous-ness. These facts are declared in verse 5: "For we through the Spirit wait for the hope of righteousness by faith." "Through the Spirit" can be misleading. There is no definite article, and as on many other occasions in Paul's writings, notably Romans 7 and 8, the spirit denotes that which is inward, the new man, the inner man, the law of the mind. By spirit, or in spirit, with minds enlightened, and hearts attuned by God's saving truth, they waited for righteousness which would come to them through faith. Here Paul has the goal princi-pally in view. Righteousness is a crown bestowed upon those who love Christ's appearing: not a crown *for* righteousness, a crown which *is* righteousness (2 Timothy 4:8). In a sense "righteousness" is now the possession of the believer: for

Christ "is made unto us wisdom, and righteousness, and sanctification, and redemption" (1 Corinthians 1:30). "The Gentiles, which followed not after righteousness, have attained to righteousness, even the righteousness which is of faith" (Romans 9:30). This righteousness is reckoned to them by God; and, springing out of "the faith" upon which man exercises his faith, comes a seeking after God and His righteousness. There is a following after righteousness: a hungering and thirsting for it, which qualify those so exercised for receiving a nature in which righteousness is as natural as sin is to the present state.

Paul steps forward in his explanation, and concludes it, by saying, "For in Jesus Christ neither circumcision availeth any thing, nor uncircumcision: but faith which worketh by love." Abraham's circumcision followed his acceptance; Paul's preceded it: but in neither case did circumcision contribute anything to faith. A cutting off of flesh did not motivate life, and men "in Christ" knew it: by experience they knew the power of faith to promote love and to express itself in love, both to God and man.

Here we might observe a corrective to a modern wrong emphasis. Faith today is discounted and love is extolled. The divine way makes faith the basis—a faith which is not passive but which expresses itself in love. Love is the instrument and at the same time the end of faith: "The end of the commandment is love out of a pure heart, and of a good conscience, and of faith unfeigned" (1 Timothy 1:5).

"Ye were running well"—it is the voice of a teacher who has watched their progress and rejoiced in it, but who is now troubled about them, and seeking to win them to the old paths. He is urging them to this, but someone else was putting obstacles in their way and so hindering them—and it may be, since Paul asks, "Who is *he*?" that Paul is thinking of the one leading teacher, perhaps the single teacher whose subtle influence had led them astray—the one described as "he that troubleth you". Paul asks them who he is in order to assess his worth, his doctrine, his aim, and the issue of his work. Paul describes his influence as hindering "that ye should obey (the) truth". The absence of the definite article in the better manuscripts throws emphasis upon the fact that what they were refusing was truth—not a set of doctrines viewed objectively as "the truth", but that which, since it contrasts with the type, was the reality, the substance. It indirectly indicates that it was but shadow to which they were turning. Since God had established "truth" in Jesus

(Ephesians 4:21), their turning to law could not be of God who had called them to the gospel and therefore the false teacher could not be divinely sent.

If the teaching was false there should be no parley: for false teaching is like leaven, gradually pervading the whole by a subtle penetrating influence. Paul uses what appears to be a proverb — "A little leaven leaveneth the whole lump" — and the figure is a warning against despising the small beginnings of an evil. Here used of doctrine, the proverb occurs again in 1 Corinthians 5:6 where it is used of gross sin. In both cases a grave warning is uttered and the eradication of the evil enjoined.

Paul expects that his counsel will prevail. He does not give them up: "I have confidence in you through the Lord, that ye will be none otherwise minded: but he that troubleth you shall bear his judgement, whosoever he be" (verse 10). The reference to judgement is a solemn thought which all teachers should bear in mind. "Be not many teachers", says James, "knowing that we shall receive the greater condemnation." Men who teach multiply themselves for good or evil in the disciples, and one who assists in forming the mind of another rightly sustains a responsibility for his work. The judgement is seen now in measure, but it is doubtless to a future day that both Paul and James refer. With the thought of the teacher's responsibility in mind Paul adds: "And I, brethren, if I yet preach circumcision, why do I yet suffer persecution? then is the offence of the cross ceased." If, as the Judaizers had claimed, Paul vacillated and preached circumcision, why did they persecute him? Their very hatred of Paul shows a difference between them in doctrine which was fundamental. The charge was false, therefore, and since the premise in the statement is false, the conclusion about the offence of the cross having ceased is satirical. Only too well, and with good reason did Paul know that it remained. He understood the attitude of his enemies, for he had once shared their view. But the irresistible evidence to which he had fully yielded only revealed in the case of the rejecters of Christ how stubborn were their hearts. The "offence of the cross" was not that Christ died on a stake; nor yet that in his death Christ exhibited a submission to evil which sets forth a pattern to others; the "offence" is in the fact that God has decreed that only by that death could His own righteousness be declared and men attain to His righteousness by the justification which comes from faith in Christ crucified.

103

The RV margin of verse 12—"I would they would even mutilate themselves"—is a translation approved by the unanimous opinion of the ancient Greek commentators. Why do they not, says Paul, since they have such faith in the knife, practice the complete mutilation which was common among the devotees of Cybele? In modern times this interpretation has been rejected on the ground of coarseness, but if we remember that in turning to Judaism the Galatians were virtually turning back in principle to the rite of the nature worship of their pagan days, and also remember the satirical touch in the words preceding, then Paul's words practically mean that if the Judaizer was leading them back, then let him consistently go the whole way and in mutilation of self exhibit in symbol the destruction of self in the complete sense.

It might lastly be noted that Paul uses a strong word to describe these opponents. They were hinderers (verse 7); they are now troublers—the word which is used of Paul's activities at Thessalonica: "turned the world upside down". Such is a seditious act subversive of true and ordered government: and that describes the position of any exponent of a false doctrine.

## LIBERTY IS NOT LICENCE (5:13–15)

MEN are always prone to extremes, opposing one extreme statement by its opposite; and some swing, pendulum-like, from one untenable view to an equally untenable view. Error often arises from an over emphasis of one aspect of doctrine while another aspect is overlooked. Truth is comprehensive, with every feature of doctrine in balanced proportion. Both in doctrine and in practice therefore truth is discerned when every feature is given its proper place and emphasis. For example, Jesus was neither God the Son nor a mere man; he was both son of God and son of man. Again, liberty is not licence, neither is restraint bondage. True freedom is shown in a self-regulated life guided by holiness of truth.

In the conflict of thought that raged in the first century, when ideas were in a state of flux, some specious arguments were advanced to justify an abandonment to all kinds of immoral acts. Hints of such perversions may be found in the epistles. In Christ God's grace is manifested for the forgiveness of sins. The one sin of Adam involved all his posterity in the consequences of his one act: but the grace of God abounds in that many offences are forgiven because of Christ's obedience. This is apostolic teaching; then comes the seductive carnal suggestion: if we multiply offences then God's grace will have opportunity to abound the more! When Paul asks the question in Romans 6:1: "Shall we keep on sinning that grace may abound?" he was not raising a remote academic point, but dealing with a very practical issue raised by teachers to such errors. So far did these unspiritual men go that Jude says they "turned the grace of God into lasciviousness". Another aspect of the same error lay in the view that the flesh was inherently evil and therefore any fleshly acts left untouched the spiritual man, and whatever vice he practised left him free from sin. As John says, any who thus argued deceived themselves. Some in Corinth were quick to misuse Paul's claim that "all things were lawful" and to work out a series of analogies which culminated in a justification of an immoral life (1 Corinthians 6:12–18).

Paul uses the word liberty more frequently in Galatians than in any other epistle. He has called the Galatians to stand fast in the liberty that belongs to the sons of God. Paul's opponents made the charge that his teaching practically made a man free from law. This was false, but it expressed a real danger in that his teaching could be so perverted.

Apart from philosophies, good or bad, liberty can have dangers. Freedom suddenly conferred on those untrained in its use can bring disaster. Freedom has its responsibilities and its temptations; it is not for children who have not yet learned the self-control that discipline brings, nor yet for adults who by mental defect are incapable of using it aright. On the one side the Galatians have been told of their privileges in Christ: they were heirs of the promises, adopted sons of God. God had called them and they had learned that "the Lord knoweth them that are his": that therefore they could call Him "Abba, Father" (4:6). They had also to learn that "everyone that nameth the name of the Lord" must "depart from iniquity" (2 Timothy 2:19). With the two aspects recognised, then, as Paul elsewhere said, "The foundation of the Lord standeth sure".

These two sides of the matter brought thus together by Paul in 2 Timothy 2, were illustrated in the episode of the rebellion of Korah and his company. They demanded freedom to exercise the office of Moses and Aaron, who were charged with taking too much upon themselves. The whole nation had been delivered from bondage, but that did not make them free to seek everything upon which their soul was set. God had delivered them that they might serve Him, and serve Him in the way He laid down. Moses, aghast at the presumption, declared that God would show on the morrow *"who are his"*, and this was done in a divinely effectual way in the earth's engulfing of the rebels. But before this judgement fell a call was made, *"Depart from the tents of these wicked men"*, and those who did found safety. Here then in Numbers 16:5 and 26, is the basis of the twofold saying which sets forth the divine blessing and the human responsibility in Paul's words to Timothy.

Korah and his company were still slaves and therefore not fit for true freedom. "He that committeth sin is the slave of sin", Jesus said. And the sin of the soul which never finds expression in outward act is as enslaving as that which is evident to all. Sin deceives as well as enslaves: and when the first enthusiasm for life in Christ has somewhat spent itself and the old life begins to assert itself again it is a plausible allurement that since there is forgiveness, the sin may be indulged. It was therefore no idle counsel when Paul instructed his readers that their freedom did not permit self-indulgence: "Use not liberty for an occasion of the flesh", and we should remember "flesh" stands for the whole natural man, whose works as set out in verses 19–21 cover the range of human activity. But negative advice is less than half of needed counsel, and it is Paul's way to give the more important positive by which the error is overcome or eradicated. Hence he adds: "but by love serve one another".

In this paradox of the slavery of love they would find true freedom. Legalism belongs to the domain of the intellect; and the legalist is an adherent of the law of works by which no flesh is justified. In fact, as we have previously found (see 3:10,11), his very way of approach fosters pride and so sin. The legalist if sincere becomes the Pharisee; if insincere the hypocrite; and in either case is not approved of God or a blessing to men. But love introduces another factor on another level of being. Bible love is not merely a sentiment as many seem to think, but it does touch the heart and the emotions. The Biblical love is not a feeling, but something moved by the will, moving the heart in the required direction. Love involves loyalty and is the mark of a personal relationship. Jesus emphasised how misconceived was the Pharisee's view of the Law when he said that the whole law consisted of two commandments—love of God with soul and heart and strength, and of neighbours as oneself. The Law was kept as God wanted it to be observed when such an attitude to Himself and to men moved all their efforts to keep the commandments. These then define the channels along which love should flow.

To suggest that a man could sin that grace might abound is a denial of the high personal relationship established by grace. To be united with Christ who died and rose again is to be joined to the one who did not sin. And the grace expressed in him is not an excuse for sin but a reason for sin being eschewed.

"By love be enslaved to one another"—so doing, the desire to be under law would be fully satisfied; for the law "was fulfilled in one word, even in this: Thou shalt love thy neighbour as thyself" (verse 14). This command is found in Leviticus 19 among "sundry laws", covering a wide range of duties; and in such a context the reason why they should not hate in their heart, or grudge, or avenge, was because a man should love his neighbour as himself. Such a vital comprehensive commandment is tucked away in the midst of many details because God's law is one, and the detail is the expression of the principle. There are no gradations of duties, some important, others of little consequence, because failure in any is failure in love.

As love brings peace, so legalism leads to strife. The effect of the false teaching had produced bickering and contention, making ecclesial life like a jungle where beasts ravin and tear. Paul therefore is content merely to state the condition and consequence of such who were ensnared: "But if ye bite and devour one another, take heed that ye be not consumed one of another." Self-destruction follows inward strife; biters need muzzling; devourers need chains. What a mistaken freedom that called for such control! The despotism of law that they wished to enthrone produced the anarchy of wild life. The gospel of God's grace gave the freedom of godly self-control.

THE SPIRITUAL AND THE CARNAL (5:16–24)

BY what means can men avoid the mutual destruction indicated in verse 15? The answer is given in a short survey of the antagonist forces at work in a Christian, with guidance on the way to ensure that the spiritual shall triumph. These opposing influences are described by the words "spirit" and "flesh", but the use and misuse of the capital letter in the former word has in some measure contributed to the misunderstanding of Paul's meaning. "Spirit" is an important word with a variety of meanings, the underlying connections being traceable, but all need not be followed out here. "God is a spirit", said Jesus; the power of God is called spirit, and that power in special manifestation is called Holy Spirit. "My words are spirit and they are life", Jesus declared. The spirit is invisible yet powerful, and denotes in a number of passages that which is real and permanent in contrast to the outward and passing form. By the rite of circumcision the Jew was outwardly declared to be such; but there was also another Jew—a son of Abraham by faith—whose circumcision was of the heart, and who therefore is called a Jew inwardly. The outward sign was a symbol of the cutting away of the fleshly desires, but the symbol was borne by many who made no effort to translate the symbol into action. On the other hand a Gentile who fulfilled the essential meaning of the rite, though without the outward sign, was more truly a Jew than the other. So Paul reasons in Romans 2:25–29.

In the passage under consideration we have once more a parallel with the letter to the Romans, chapters 7 and 8. There Paul speaks of "sin working in me"; "in me (that is, in my flesh) dwelleth no good thing"; "a law—evil present with me"; "a law in my members", and a one word synonym is the "flesh". In contrast to these descriptions of the forces opposed to God's will, we have an "I" that does not consent, a "will" that is present, an "inward man", "my mind"—and with this, says Paul, "I myself serve the law of God". As we pass to the eighth chapter the antonyms used are "flesh" and "spirit"—the latter taking the place of "my mind".

The "flesh" describes the individual actuated by the impulses which spring from the flesh and which have a bias away from God, a bent to go contrary to the will of God. This is the heritage of all the sons of Adam. It is beyond the power of flesh to lift itself to a higher level, and any energy moving towards divine standards must therefore come from without. If man's freedom remains unaffected the new force must take the form of ideas by which a man is instructed and urged towards a life conformable to God's will. Such a mode of thinking is derivable only from God's word, and this received in faith and humility is capable of transforming a person by renewing his mind. In *Elpis Israel*, Dr. Thomas gathers together from the word of God some of the descriptions of this reformed way of thinking in harmony with God's revelation.

"This new mode of thinking and feeling created in a true believer by the divine law and testimony, is variously designated in scripture. It is styled 'a clean heart and a right spirit'; 'a new spirit' and 'a heart of flesh'; the 'inward man';

'new creature'; 'the new man created in righteousness and true holiness'; and 'renewed unto knowledge after the image of him that created him'; the 'hidden man of the heart'; and so forth. This new and hidden man is manifested in the life, which is virtuous as becomes the gospel. He delights in the law of the Lord, and speaks often of His testimonies. He denies himself of all ungodliness and worldly lusts, and walks soberly, righteously and godly in the world. His hope is the glorious manifestation of Jesus Christ, with the crown of righteousness, even glory, honour, and immortality, promised to all who look for him, and 'love his appearing', and desire his kingdom."

Add the word "spirit" as the most important of those covered by "so forth" in the above quotation, and the reader has the data for a correct interpretation of this section of the Galatian epistle.

"Walk in spirit", says Paul, "and ye shall not fulfil the lust of the flesh." Here is the method by which fleshly ways can be avoided. As a man cannot traverse two roads going diverse ways at the same time, neither can he walk in spirit and in flesh at the same time. The idea of a walk as action along a way, which Paul so delights to use, is a figure taken from the Old Testament, illustrated by many statements in Psalms and Proverbs. "Spirit" is the environment, the condition of the life so described; it is a spiritual life. The flesh is best suppressed, not so much by the direct effort of the will to subdue it, but by the attention to and cultivation of the opposite. "Put ye on the Lord Jesus Christ, and make not provision for the flesh to fulfil the lusts thereof" (Romans 13:14). A thing unprovided for dies of starvation and neglect. This is obviously true, but so definite a statement can be an over-simplification of the matter. In fact "flesh" and "spirit" are both ever present together in the man of God; the "spirit" needs cultivation and is not native; the flesh is in occupation. Therefore the conflict is never a complete victory of the spirit, and sometimes almost seems a defeat. Nevertheless Paul is confident that the victory is with the spirit if the cause of the spirit is espoused. His words in verse 17 are really an elaboration of the thought of "not fulfilling the desires of the flesh" of verse 16; admitting indeed that the "adversaries" are at grips, but declaring "the spirit" is the victor. "For the flesh", says Paul, "lusteth against the Spirit, and the Spirit against the flesh: and these are contrary the one to the other: so that ye cannot do the things that ye would." The last phrase, "do the things that ye would", has been given two different interpretations;

first that the flesh overcomes and we fail to do what we would but, second, that because the spirit is powerful it succeeds, and we do not yield to the things the flesh would have us do. The latter is in keeping with the tone of confidence in the passage, and also fits the context both before and after; for Paul continues as if the spirit was triumphant: "But if ye be led of the Spirit, ye are not under the law".

The true antithesis here would be, that being led by the spirit they were not under the flesh: but while Paul means that, he also by changing the words says much more. The fleshly antagonism is evoked by the Law, as the apostle has shown: the power of the flesh rests on law: and therefore law cannot bring men to salvation. To be led by the spirit is therefore not only a conquest of flesh, but is an adoption of the way of God's salvation by the gospel of grace and not by law. In following the spirit they were not seeking by the Law to attain to salvation: and therefore as followers of the true way of life were not under the Law. Under the Spirit's guidance and rule all fleshly achievements were discounted, and they did not come under the Law as a source of direction, or of condemnation.

In verses 19–21 Paul unveils the character of fleshly "works"; in verse 22 the "fruit" of the spirit. Works are activities, and since they are forbidden by the Law and yet revealed by law, the use of the word "works" here may be suggested by the "law" in verse 18; as though Paul said, "You seek to excel by works of law; these are the works that the law shows to be the production of the flesh". "Fruit" is cultivated by care and patience, by wise husbandry; it comes by growth and marks maturity.

There are many gross evils in human life which are usually hidden from view, works of flesh and of darkness in every sense. But the flesh is equally active in many other exercises than the carnal vices: in wrath, strife, sedition, revellings which are more openly displayed. But there are inner desires such as idolatry, emulations, envyings, which also spring from flesh. No age has a monopoly of any of the things named, and no age is without every evil named.

The fruit—for it is one fruit—consists of "love, joy, peace, longsuffering, gentleness, goodness, faith, meekness, temperance". There is no law against such things. The law which had the power of stirring up the flesh has no power to prevent the cultivation of spiritual things. While law aims at restraint in its normal operation, in spiritual things nothing calls for repression.

110

It is evident that Paul is pointing to something more effective than the mere acknowledgment of law. Men limited to law as the horizon of life were so shut in by it that the horizon narrowed to a prison house. What was needed was a new motive power for righteousness. Paul himself had found this power in Christ Jesus: "I can do all things through Christ who strengtheneth me." He had seen the flesh for what it was; he had come to understand how it was repudiated in the act of Jesus in submitting to crucifixion. He had recognised the necessity of identifying himself with that death of Jesus so that in a sense it became his death: "I am crucified with Christ." Thus sharing that death Paul also shared in Christ's resurrection in that in Christ he rose to a newness of life. "If we have been planted together in the likeness of his death, we shall be also in the likeness of his resurrection; knowing this, that our old man is crucified with him that the body of sin might be destroyed, that henceforth we should not serve sin" (Romans 6:5,6). A new centre of power is established by this allegiance to Christ, and even though the old habits persist with weakened power, and though there is repeated failure to reach the desired standard, yet the old habit centres have been broken, to be gradually overcome. The acceptance of Christ as Saviour is at the same time a repudiation of the claims of sin to be master. Christ is accepted as Lord with such a personal devotion that active motives and powers for holiness take the dominant position formerly held by fleshly desires. They that are Christ's "have crucified the flesh with the affections and lusts" (verse 24).

## CARE FOR OTHERS (5:25—6:5)

THE new life in Christ affects a person individually and socially; for not only has he become related to Christ but also to those in Christ. The new spirit guides a man's actions and governs his relations with others. The whole of the believers are so knit together that their relationship to Christ and to each other is described by the figures of the vine, and of the human body. Christ is the vine, they are the branches; Christ is the head, they are members of his body. In verse 16 Paul had spoken of "walking in spirit", the reference being to the individual walk in the way of life. In verse 25 he uses another word (but translated by the same English word) which denotes a walk in relation to others: "to walk in line"; hence the idea of marching, and with perhaps the suggestion of discipline that is involved in its use as a military term. "If we live in the Spirit", if the new life is our personal environment,

111

then "let us also march in spirit"; let our united activities be animated by the same principles.

The harmonious association indicated in verse 25 naturally leads to the counsel not to cultivate the opposite: "Let us not be desirous of vain glory, provoking one another, envying one another". The quality of an army depends very much on the spirit that animates officers and ranks. There is a duty of loyalty, of helpfulness, and this is seen in the attitude to the weak and the sick. Every effort is made on their behalf that they are not left to the enemy. Perhaps some such thought is the connecting link with the counsel in 6:1 concerning a transgressor: "Brethren, if a man be overtaken in a fault, ye which are spiritual, restore such an one in the spirit of meekness: considering thyself, lest thou also be tempted." The duty to an erring member laid down in this command is in keeping with the Lord's teaching. If a man trespass against another, the Lord puts the responsibility of seeking the amendment of the wrong doer upon the offended party. In many cases, in the first instance, he alone knows of the fault; and instead of taking umbrage and seeking redress, the Lord requires that he take steps to remove the fault of the other by personal interview first, and then if that fails with the aid of others. Matthew 18:15–20 is not rightly interpreted as a sanction for exacting a penalty or even redress from a wrongdoer; it is a solemn and serious statement of duty towards an offender with a view to his recovery from his sin. Jesus puts in a terrible light the action which causes another to sin: "Better to be drowned than be guilty of that", says Jesus. If the disciple recognises that putting a stumbling block in another's way is so grievous a fault, then the commands "to rebuke" and "to forgive" follow as a reasonable duty (Luke 17:1–5). Admittedly this is hard, as the apostles recognised at once, saying, "Lord, increase our faith."

If a man be detected in a fault an effort has to be made for his recovery, "to restore him". We use the word "restore" when we speak of a person who has been sick being restored to health; transgression is like a sickness and an effort has to be made to restore a transgressor to spiritual health. The word translated "restore" is used of mending nets (Matthew 4:21), of "preparing" the body of Messiah (Hebrews 10:5), of "making perfect" (Hebrews 13:21—where observe not only the repetition of this word from 10:5, but also the recurrence of "will"; 1 Peter 5:10), of "fitting" vessels of wrath for destruction (Romans 9:22), and of the perfect joining together in one mind and one judgement, which leads to speaking the same things and so avoiding "schisms" (1 Corinthians 1:10). The word describes the reconciling of contending factions; the replacing of a dislocated joint; or the repair of a torn fabric. There is in each case readjustment, that a thing may be fitted for the end the user has in view.

What can be done to "restore" a man spiritually sick? What steps can be taken to bring about recovery? There is a difference between the natural and the spiritual. In a normal body during the greater part of life there are latent forces ready to work for recovery of wounds or fractures or diseased parts. But the spiritual in man depends upon his accepting resources outside himself. A man more readily perceives his bodily ill-health than his soul's sickness, for sin deceives and ever seeks to camouflage the sin and disguise its real shape.

Yet recovery waits for the recognition of the fault, its confession, its pursuit of forgiveness, both human and divine. Here is a task for wise men, and this Paul recognises. He calls upon "ye that are spiritual" to engage in the task. A natural man cannot diagnose the things of the spirit, neither does he discern the required "treatment". But a spiritual man, conscious that a soul's salvation is involved, feels his insufficiency. Arrogance or pride would hinder the work: "the spirit of meekness" must mark the physicians, while each contributor to the work keeps in mind the proneness of everyone to fall when tempted.

"Bear ye one another's burdens and so fulfil the law of Christ" is a command that springs from the duty defined in verse 1. It states in general form a duty of which verse 1 is a particular application. "Love thy neighbour as thyself" was the very essence of the law both of Moses and of Christ: but Jesus expressed it also in another form: "As ye would that men should do to you, do ye also to them." But Jesus embodied the rule in his own life, and because of his perfect obedience in all things he was raised to life. This work was the work of the Messiah as required by Old Testament prophecy, and it is noteworthy that Paul does not say the law which Jesus spake, but "fulfil the law of Christ", the law of the Messiah. That law is the law of his life, and to fulfil the law of the Messiah is to sustain a personal relationship to him which moves a person to serve others. The injunction in Romans 15:1–3 binds the believer to Christ in one service of seeking the good of neighbour, and the thought of these verses might be treated as an expansion of Galatians 6:2. They read:

"We then that are strong ought to bear the infirmities of the weak, and not to please ourselves. Let every one of us please his neighbour for his good to edification. For even Christ pleased not himself; but, as it is written, The reproaches of them that reproached thee fell on me."

(Romans 15:1–3)

If a person is not willing to serve he is blinded by pride and self-deceived. By thinking himself to be something, he shows he is nothing (verse 3). Hence the counsel that a man "prove" his work: he must weigh his own actions; for in a satisfactory result of such examination and not in any comparison with another is there ground for rejoicing. There can be no shifting of personal responsibility; a man cannot feel himself approved because he, like the Pharisee, thinks himself different from other men. At last every man gives account of his own stewardship. This responsibility is expressed in a graphic figure, which is obscured in translation by the repetition of the words "bearing burdens" which introduces confusion between verses 2 and 5. In the former, the burdens are the cares of life which can be shared: in the latter it can be the personal load of the soldier for which he is responsible, or the cargo of a ship. Life is like a trading enterprise, and when the ships all enter harbour it will be the cargo each carries that will be examined for approval. Everyone must give account for his own actions. At that time each shipmaster will be less exercised about the cargo line of another than of the contents of his own hold. Transfer of trading results will be impossible; and each man must give his own report.

## DOING GOOD (6:6–10)

THE division of the epistle at verse 5 follows the paragraph arrangement of the RV although some connect verse 6 more closely with verse 5. The sixth verse takes up the thought of verse 2 about bearing one another's burdens, and the opening word "but" (RV) introduces a contrast; if the contrast is with verse 5, then Paul is saying that while responsibility is individual in the final issue, in present relationships there is not only community of faith, but also of opportunity to do good. The general exhortation contrasts with the individual warning.

The usual interpretation of the verse is that the instructed in the gospel are enjoined to support their teachers in temporal things. It implies that there were men who devoted much or the whole of their time in the oral instruction of the brethren and sisters—the word "instructed" is the original of the word "catechumen". Paul recognised a right to receive help in temporal things for the ministering of spiritual things, although he himself was jealous of his independence, accepting willing gifts from those whose benefactions sprang from grateful love, while being careful not to receive from others. The following passages bear upon the matter: 1 Corinthians 9:11; 2 Corinthians 11:7; Philippians 4:10; 1 Thessalonians 2:6,9; 1 Timothy 5:17,18.

The very basis of the Christian life is an understanding of God's purpose and His will. When manuscripts were few and teaching was largely from memory, oral instruction played a larger part than when each member had his own copy of the Scriptures. But the evident need from the earliest days that each ecclesia should have a copy of the gospels and of the epistles would call for wider distribution of these than is often recognised; and, we believe, in the case of the first three gospels, for an earlier date for their production than is usually attached to them. Nevertheless the part played by the spirit-guided teachers in the ecclesias of the early years of the apostles' labours must have been very important.

No system of instruction prevailed in pagan religions. Ritual and not faith or conduct was the means of favour; and the ritual was turned to a lucrative profession by the priests. Men had to pay for their services in approaching the god and securing the favour of the god. In Asia Minor at one time the priesthoods were put up for auction, an indication of the valuable returns such appointments could give. The worshipper was ready to pay, much as a Roman Catholic pays for masses, because certain benefits were thought to be obtainable. If a teacher gave time to instruction to the detriment of his daily work he was therefore deserving of a share in the "carnal things" of the instructed. The latter was helped to attain eternal benefits: it was a small matter that he should recompense with temporal things.

Although the above is the general interpretation of Paul's words, it may be doubted whether they represent his meaning; the important word "communicate" is used in the sense of giving to others. But the word means to take part with or be a partner with another in some activity or possession. "All good things" in which they had to share can be good actions as well as good food. The injunction then is that all, whether teachers or taught, must work together as partners in doing good, in bearing each other's burdens (verse 2), in helping the erring (verse 1). The mutual activity in good works, whether

115

helping in carnal things, in ecclesial duties, or in spiritual comfort, is an effective remedy for the disaffection and self-sufficiency referred to in verse 3.

Whichever view of verse 6 be adopted there is no mistaking the general lesson of verses 7 and 8:

"Be not deceived: God is not mocked; for whatsoever a man soweth, that shall he also reap. For he that soweth to his flesh shall of the flesh reap corruption; but he that soweth to the Spirit shall of the Spirit reap life everlasting."

A man who is selfish and sows sparingly reaps sparingly. A piety that is confined to profession is a pretence, and makes an offering to God which is counterfeit. The offerer may deceive himself—hence the warning; for God is not mocked, and God's law rules. "The liberal deviseth liberal things, and by liberal things shall he stand." It is a rule easily learnt from the natural world: grapes are not gathered from thorns; and men who sow wickedness reap the same. Sowing and reaping in the natural belong to the present. The sluggard who does not plough because of the cold, has no harvest at the end of the season. The man who allows weeds their way, will not reap good crops. But men's actions not only influence the present, but are related to the future when God bestows His rewards. To the responsible man the day of the divine harvesting will declare what his sowing has been.

There are two kinds of sowing—actions are related to two fields of life: the flesh and the spirit. A man sows to the flesh when he serves himself, when his life is lived for self and the gratification of every desire. Flesh belongs to the present, to the temporal order, to that which passes. There is no prospect of any eternal results from flesh; as water cannot rise higher than its source, neither can flesh produce anything having the quality of permanence. Things of the flesh all pass. The spirit, as we have seen, is used in chapter 5 of the new life in Christ, and this new life springs from the incorruptible seed, the word of God, which liveth and abideth for ever (1 Peter 1:23).

The newness of life, if persevered in and nurtured, produces a character having in God's mercy some basis for perpetuation. In God's mercy—for we cannot earn life, but we can so follow after righteousness that when the crown of righteousness is bestowed it will be a welcome, an appreciated, and an understood gift. The carnal man who farms the flesh, would feel a stranger in the spiritual world. But a spiritual life now will be found to have been a needful preparation for eternal life which will be bestowed in the day when God judges the secrets of men by Jesus Christ.

Since the flesh is ever there with persistent demands, the spiritual can flag if not encouraged. The apostle puts the certainty of the future reward as inducement to perseverance in good. "Let us not be weary in well doing: for in due season we shall reap, if we faint not." With the Lord in mind as the harvester, with the assurance of results from good sowing, the counsel concludes with the appropriate words: "So then as we have opportunity, let us work that which is good toward all men, and especially toward them that are of the household of faith."

# SECTION 5

## CONCLUSION — THE AUTOGRAPH (6:11–18)
### "SEE HOW LARGE LETTERS I HAVE WRITTEN ..."

WITH these opening words Paul begins his closing section: and a large field for speculation they have afforded those who have tried to interpret Paul. The advocates of the theory that Paul suffered from deficient sight consequent upon his vision of the risen Lord find here one of the proofs, surmising that he had written the whole letter himself in clumsy letters. Deissmann finds in the words a jocular comment, as of a schoolmaster with children with whom he has been cross, a suggestion rightly stigmatised by Ramsay as "the region of pure comedy".

It might be noticed first that it was Paul's practice after dictating a letter to an amanuensis to add an autograph benediction. "The salutation of me Paul, with mine own hand, which is the token in every epistle" (2 Thessalonians 3:17). "The salutation of me, Paul, with mine own hand. Remember my bonds. Grace be with you" (Colossians 4:18). See also 1 Corinthians 16:21. Even when there is not so specific a reference to Paul's own handwriting, guided by his statement that it was his usual practice we can feel sure that the closing words of some of the other letters were penned by Paul himself.

Paul, then, at verse 11, took pen in hand, and in larger letters wrote his concluding words. That such was unusual is clear from the fact that he draws attention to it. What bearing had it upon these last words? Ramsay points to examples from Pisidian Antioch and Pompeii of a custom of emphasising an important point in an inscription by using larger letters. The printer's art is used in a similar way today in displayed advertisements. If that is the case, are the concluding sentences of the letter such as might be so emphasised? We find they are a summary of what he has been saying throughout the epistle, and very fittingly might be given such an emphasis. The language is direct and focuses the issue in few words.

The Judaizers are first accused of being limited to a fleshly outlook. "As many as desire to make a fair show in the flesh, they compel you to be circumcised." There was no recognition of spiritual values; they thought only of the outward, of the rite and not its significance. Paul then gives their motive. Their attitude did not spring from love of the Law, but "only that they may not be persecuted for the cross of Christ". Evidently the Judaizers feared persecution for believing in Christ crucified; it was not an imaginary danger, as Paul's own experience shows. But by urging circumcision as well as belief of the gospel, the ground of Jewish hatred was removed. They were thus more concerned with what men thought of them than how God regarded them; they wanted to secure the future but not at present hardship. All this is but a fleshly show.

The Judaizers were inconsistent. Since their proselytes to circumcision were living in disregard of the law, their life was evidently outwardly insincere. "For not even they who receive circumcision do themselves keep the law, but they desire to have you circumcised, that they may glory in your flesh" (verse 13, RV). The latter portion of the verse indicates that by compelling circumcision they would ingratiate themselves with their fellow Jews. 'Truly', they would say, 'we believe in Jesus, but the consequence is to bring Gentiles to the Jewish cause. We are proselytising and making Jewish converts of Christian disciples.' But confession of Christ was an admission that the law could not save, and to preach Christ and the law at the same time denoted an insincerity in their inner life.

Paul swept away Jewish sophistries by an emphatic statement of his own position. "But far be it from me to glory, save in the cross of our Lord Jesus Christ, through which the world hath been crucified unto me, and I unto the world" (verse 14).

In these words Paul repudiates all personal glorying. He has learnt how powerless human efforts in themselves are to bring favour from God. To approach God on the basis of merit can only end in condemnation. But in the cross of the Lord Jesus Christ (observe the full title) the flesh had been repudiated and God exalted. The world (and it was the Jewish world that demanded the death of Jesus) had revealed its basic antagonism to God, as Jesus by his life and death had manifested his willing assent to God's decrees. The world being thus revealed for what it really is, must be put to death; and so far as Paul was concerned, since the example of Jesus showed that the flesh must be crucified, Paul will regard the world of flesh as a felon finding a fitting end on the cross. The power of the world over him thus came to an end; and since he was crucified with Christ his own desire for worldly things had been done away. To men the world is the expression of the real, and they render it honour and submit to its bondage. In fact, it is passing, but it deludes its worshippers. But Christ's death revealed its mocking power; and the man crucified with Christ passes from its power and sees its glory to be tinsel, and its service to be slavery. God is the reality and His service is the only basis of permanent good. Paul in the richness of his thought thinks of three crosses. Christ, the world, and Paul, are all crucified. Yet only Christ is crucified, but in accepting Christ Paul is crucified with him, and the flesh (the basis of the world) is crucified in Paul. Paul's language then is a definition of his personal experience. The only place and cause of glorying is in a crucified Christ; to glory in anything else is to glory in a world that has been sentenced in that very act of the world in crucifying Jesus.

What is a mere cutting in flesh against such a scene? Neither is circumcision anything, nor uncircumcision. They belong to outward passing things: neither has regenerative power; both leave a man morally neither better nor worse. But in Christ crucified an old world perishes that a new might be born; and as Christ rose to newness of life, so men "planted in the likeness of his death" rise to a newness of life, becoming "new creatures" by God's grace. Here is regeneration, but it is through God's work in Christ, and it is to be found nowhere else. Apart from this, and outside of this, men are away from God, strangers to covenant blessings, fleshly rejects. With Christ, walking according to this rule that the flesh profits nothing and only God's regeneration in His only begotten Son avails, men find there is peace and mercy, for they are the Israel of God—the true overcomers and prevailers, the inheritors of the blessings and the promises, the princes with God.

The tone of the seventeenth verse is stern; it must be read with all the earnest and emotional pleadings of the last two chapters of the letter in mind. Undoubtedly it is a strong assertion of his authority as an apostle, and that what he has written is not something about which they could enter into argument. "From henceforth let no man trouble me." There are occasions when striving must cease; even lesser men than Paul, and without his authority, feel at times that all has been said that profitably can be. There are men ever learning and never able to come to the knowledge of the truth. There

121

are circumstances when the duties of building up and strengthening faithful men and women in Christ must take precedence; then the words of Paul to the Corinthians, "If any man be ignorant, let him be ignorant" (1 Corinthians 14:38), take on a meaning not fully perceived in other circumstances. It belongs to apostolic authority to say, " If any man love not the Lord Jesus Christ, let him be Anathema, The Lord cometh"; but its meaning is understood the better when the troubles discussed in the epistle concluded by those words, have been understood (1 Corinthians 16:22). If any in Galatia wished to be contentious then it was not with Paul they would strive. He had given an authoritative answer: and the note with which the letter began is heard again at its close.

He reminds them, however, why he could so speak: "for I bear branded in my body the marks of the Lord Jesus". At Antioch he had suffered "persecution" which led to his expulsion from the city. Such official action would almost certainly be accompanied with a beating from the lictors who attended the magistrates. At Lystra he was stoned. The marks and scars of these and other sufferings endured for Christ's sake Paul compares to the branding which slaves bore. Such stigmata were evidence of a master's title, or that the slave was attached to some temple worship which in turn afforded certain protection. Paul was the bondslave of Christ, of that the words clearly bear witness whatever precise meaning Paul had in mind. He calls these marks the stigmata of the Lord Jesus—or with RV simply Jesus. This latter lends colour to the idea that Paul is thinking of a correspondence between his marks and the wound prints in the hands and feet of Jesus. In the sustained paradoxes in 2 Corinthians 4 he speaks of "bearing about in the body the putting to death of Jesus, that the life of Jesus may be manifested in our body" (verse 10); and in Colossians 1:24 he speaks of the "afflictions of Christ" filled up in his sufferings. If these thoughts were present in his mind here, then the reference to the "branding" catches up the idea he had more than once expressed of being crucified with Christ. Both ideas were a powerful reminder to the Galatians of the way they had received him as a messenger of God.

The benediction is brief but strikingly appropriate. "The grace of our Lord Jesus Christ be with your spirit, brethren" (RV). "Grace", the full titles of Jesus, the use of "spirit" for "you" recalling the use of the word earlier in the epistle, and lastly, the word "brethren", gather in a valediction the epistle's message.

So ends the first great struggle for the "truth in Jesus" in the Christian era. For we may be sure it did end the strife in Galatia, just as the whole controversy on the Jewish law in its bearing upon Christians came to an end. The form of heresy changes, but the essential principles of truth do not change. The Galatian epistle, therefore, though so instinct with the emotion evoked by the trouble, yet lives with its enunciation of divine principles for the generations far removed in time and space from the Galatian province of Asia Minor. The epistle has been like "living fire" again and again in quickening men to vital thinking when the deadening influence of ritual was destroying spiritual life. The epistle sustains life in the spirit to all in every land and time who read with understanding.

# SCRIPTURE REFERENCES

126

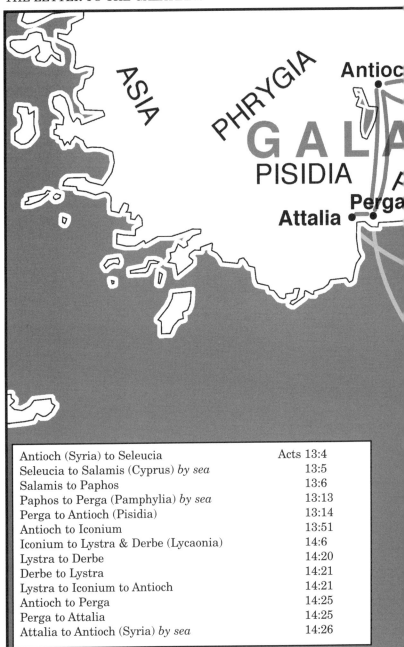

| Antioch (Syria) to Seleucia | Acts 13:4 |
| Seleucia to Salamis (Cyprus) *by sea* | 13:5 |
| Salamis to Paphos | 13:6 |
| Paphos to Perga (Pamphylia) *by sea* | 13:13 |
| Perga to Antioch (Pisidia) | 13:14 |
| Antioch to Iconium | 13:51 |
| Iconium to Lystra & Derbe (Lycaonia) | 14:6 |
| Lystra to Derbe | 14:20 |
| Derbe to Lystra | 14:21 |
| Lystra to Iconium to Antioch | 14:21 |
| Antioch to Perga | 14:25 |
| Perga to Attalia | 14:25 |
| Attalia to Antioch (Syria) *by sea* | 14:26 |

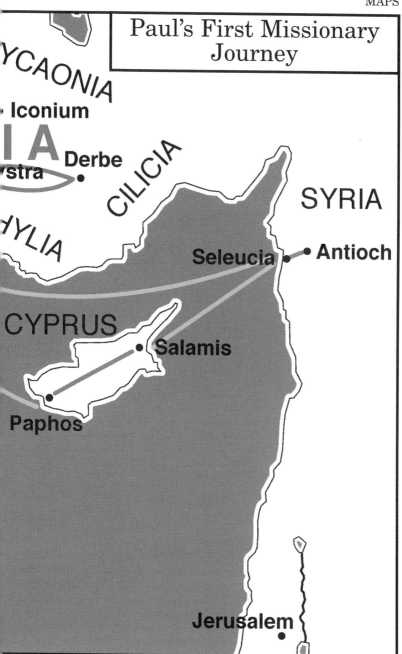

Paul's First Missionary Journey

LYCAONIA

Iconium

Derbe

stra

CILICIA

PHYLIA

SYRIA

Seleucia • Antioch

CYPRUS

Salamis

Paphos

Jerusalem

| Antioch (Syria) to Syria & Cilicia | Acts15:35,41 |
|---|---|
| Syria & Cilicia to Derbe & Lystra | 16:1 |
| Derbe & Lystra to Troas | 16:6–8 |
| Troas via Samothracia to Neapolis *by sea* | 16:11 |
| Neapolis to Philippi | 16:12 |
| Philippi via Amphipolis & Apollonia to Thessalonica | 17:1 |
| Thessalonica to Berea | 17:10 |
| Berea to Athens *by sea* | 17:15 |
| Athens to Corinth (& Cenchrea) | 18:1 (18:18) |
| Corinth to Ephesus (on route to Syria) *by sea* | 18:18,19 |
| Ephesus to Caesarea (via Rhodes & Cyprus?) *by sea* | 18:22 |
| Caesarea to Antioch | 18:22 |

# Paul's Second Missionary Journey

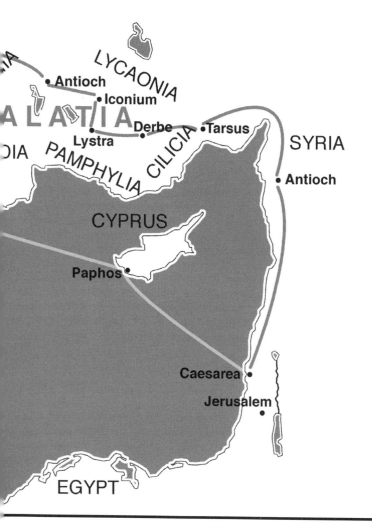

BITHYNIA AND PONTUS

LYCAONIA

• Antioch
• Iconium

ALATIA

Derbe • Tarsus

Lystra

CILICIA

PAMPHYLIA

DIA

SYRIA

• Antioch

CYPRUS

Paphos •

Caesarea •

Jerusalem •

EGYPT

| Antioch (Syria) to Galatia & Phrygia | Acts 18:22,23 |
|---|---|
| Galatia & Phrygia to Ephesus | 19:1 |
| Ephesus to Macedonia *by sea* | 20:1 |
| Macedonia to Greece | 20:2 |
| Greece to Macedonia (Philippi) | 20:3 |
| Macedonia (Philippi) to Troas *by sea* | 20:6 |
| Troas to Assos | 20:13 |
| Assos to Mitylene *by sea* | 20:14 |
| Mitylene via Chios to Samos *by sea* | 20:15 |
| Samos (Trogyllium) to Miletus | 20:15 |
| Miletus to Cos | 21:1 |
| Cos to Rhodes | 21:1 |
| Rhodes to Patara | 21:1 |
| Patara to Tyre | 21:3 |
| Tyre to Ptolemais | 21:7 |
| Ptolemais to Caesarea | 21:8 |
| Caesarea to Jerusalem | 21:15 |

# Paul's Third Missionary Journey

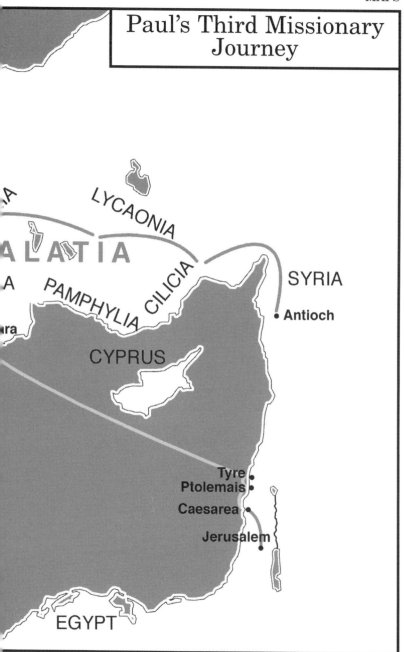